DP/08.

Salt of the Earth

A play

John Godber

D1638263

Samuel French – London
New York – Sydney – Toronto – Hollywood

ISBN 0 573 01689 5

Please see page vi for further copyright information

SALT OF THE EARTH

Commissioned by Wakefield 100, the play was first presented as part of the Wakefield Centenary celebrations at the Theatre Royal and Opera House, Wakefield, in 1988. It was subsequently rewritten and presented by the Hull Truck Theatre Company at the 1988 Edinburgh Festival, where it won a Fringe First Award, and then as part of the Perrier Pick of the Fringe Season at the Donmar Warehouse, London, with the following cast of characters:

May	Maggie Lane
Annie	Amanda Orton
Roy	Nigel Betts
Harry	William Ilkley
Paul	Nigel Betts
Kay	Julie Gibbs
Tosh	Adrian Hood
Mr Poole	Adrian Hood
Mrs Potter	Julie Gibbs
Mrs Gillespie	Julie Gibbs
Cherry	Julie Gibbs

Directed by John Godber
Designed by Robert Jones

CHARACTERS

May, Paul's mother
Annie, May's neurotic sister
Roy, Annie's husband
Harry, May's husband
Mr Poole, Pit Under-Manager
Mrs Potter, May's neighbour
Mrs Gillespie, an older woman
Paul, May and Harry's son
Kay, Paul's girl-friend
Tosh, Paul's giant of a best friend
Cherry, Paul's university girl-friend

The eleven characters in the play can be played easily by
a cast of six

The action takes place in the Yorkshire mining villages
of Upton and South Kirkby

ACT I The years 1947–1974
ACT II The years 1980–1988

CHRONOLOGY OF CHARACTERS

At the beginning of the play, 1947, May is eighteen, Annie is sixteen, Roy is seventeen and Harry is eighteen. Paul, Tosh and Kay are all born in the same year, 1956, and are aged ten when they first appear. Thus, by the end of Act I, 1974, May is forty-five, Annie is forty-three, Harry is forty-five and Paul, Tosh and Kay are eighteen. In Act II, Paul, Tosh and Kay age from twenty-four to thirty-two, May from fifty-one to sixty, Annie from forty-nine to fifty-seven and Harry from fifty-one to fifty-nine.

ACT I

West Yorkshire. 1947

The stage is pre-lit. Music: Judy Garland's recording of "The Trolley Song" plays. The House Lights go down and the Lights change to deep blue to give a night effect

Annie Parker, aged sixteen, dressed as a work girl in overalls and a headscarf, rushes on carrying a coat and a bag. She is late, and puts on her coat while calling to her sister off stage

Annie May ... May ... What's she doing now? May? Come on ... She's allus fiddling about. Come on ... what are you doing?

May Parker enters, even more untogether than Annie. She is eighteen

May I'm coming, aren't I, let me get mi things.

Annie It's fish and chip night, Fridays.

May I know.

Annie Mi dad'll never been able to keep 'em warm ont oven top.

May I hate fish and chips. I put mine in the dustbin.

Annie What have you been doing?

May Cleaning all your mess up.

Annie I didn't leave any mess.

May You did.

Annie I did not.

May You did, Annie, you left oil dripping all over the place. You've got to leave your work-tops clean, you know that. As soon as the hooter went you were off like a whippet.

Annie I don't want to miss the bus, do I?

May There's plenty of time.

Annie Not if it's full.

May We can get the next one.

Annie But I won't have time to get a bath.

May You will.

Annie But I want to soak.

May Annie, you always get carried away.

Annie I can't wait to see Roy, can you?

May What do I want to see Roy for?

Annie Well. Don't you want to see Harry?

May Not really; all we do is argue. I don't know if I even like him.

Annie I don't know what to wear.

May I haven't got much choice.

Annie I think I'll put that yellow frock on.

May Does Roy like that?

Annie I think so.

May Ask him. They're working under here. There's coal-faces all under here. (*Shouting to the miners*) Roy? Harry? Can you hear us. Are you there? Is anybody there?

Annie (*seriously*) Roy?

May She's putting that yellow frock on again, Roy. Knock twice if that's OK.

Annie Do you think they can hear us? Roy . . . It's me agen . . . I love you . . . we're going to have lots of children . . . I'll see you in the ballroom at half-seven. We're having fish and chips for tea, our May doesn't want hers. You won't be able to come home tonight because mi dad's staying in. This is Annie Parker saying: I'll see you at the Welfare.

May I wonder about you, Annie.

Annie Oh look . . .

May What?

Annie Come on . . .

They both exit at speed

The Lights change. Music: Bing Crosby singing "Piociana"

> *Two miners, Harry and Roy, crawl to the music across the stage. Harry is downstage, Roy is upstage. They have shovels and they begin shovelling together*

Harry These are our pits now tha knows, Roy. We own these buggers.

Roy Doesn't make the shovelling any bloody easier though, Harry, does it?

Harry They're our pits now, old cock, people'll always need coal, job for life, this bugger. They need us, old lad.

Roy They can have the bloody job for my money, I'm sick on it.

Harry It's a man's job, what's up wi' thee?

Roy Is it warm or am I having a bloody stroke?

Harry It's warm, we'll fill this off and then go up to Three's Junction. It's cooler.

Roy About time, I'm just about ready to drop my pants.

Harry Bloody hell, well do it down wind of me will you, my stomach's a bit dodgy as it is.

Harry continues with his shovelling. He begins to sing "If You Were the Only Boy in the World". *Roy watches him and crawls to him*

Roy Oi oi oi . . . can tha whistle?

Harry Why?

Roy Because tha can't bloody sing.

Harry Tha named the day yet?

Roy Not yet, have you?

Harry Thinking about it. Hey, have you seen their father?

Roy No.

Harry He works in the headings; they reckon he can pick up an iron-girder by hisself.

Roy Give over, I can feel thee pittling down my back.

Harry It's rate. Two men can't lift an iron-girder. Don't bloody cross him; when he says put the locker in the back wheel, put it in the back wheel.

Roy I'm getting out, tha knows, I'm not having this.

Harry What's up wi' you? It's smashing.

Roy It breaks my heart to come down here when the sun's shining.

Harry Well, when tha gets up in a morning, shut thee eyes.

Roy I'm not having this all my life.

Harry Don't you like it?

Roy Oh ay ... I like it. But there's too much fresh air for me.

Harry Has tha heard about the new under-manager?

Roy What about him?

Harry He's nine foot seven, only a young lad.

Roy Oh ay ... and has he got two heads?

Harry They reckon he's a right swine ...

Mr Poole, the under-manager, crawls to where they are working

Roy Tha going to t' Welfare "Free n' easy" toneet?

Harry Be a wonder if I don't. I haven't missed a dance in the last two years.

Roy I think they've got a new band on.

Harry They have.

Mr Poole What the bloody hell are you two doin'?

Harry We're getting this off the face as fast as we can before he shits his pants.

Mr Poole I thought you'd stopped.

Roy Are you the man they've sent from the market pool.

Harry Here grab a shovel, we need a hand, it's bloody horse-work is this. Come on here.

Roy Start down that end if you want, we'll work to meet you.

Mr Poole Do you know who I am?

Roy No.

Harry What's he say?

Roy He says, do we know who he is?

Harry I don't know who he is.

Roy Bloody hell.

Harry Poor bloke.

Roy Fancy not knowing who you are. Hey sorry, mate, I can't help you, we don't know who you are.

Mr Poole I'm the new under-manager, I'm Mr Poole.

Harry Oh bloody hell, we've done it now, Roy.

Roy Sorry, Mr Poole. For a moment there I genuinely thought you didn't know who you were.

A moment. Music: "String of Pearls". The Lights change

Everyone exits. Annie and May come on dancing

A mirror-ball spins. We are at the Miner's Welfare

May Every weekend we would dance to a new band at the Miner's Welfare.
Annie We'd put into practice the dance steps we had learnt at home.

They dance together, and fill the stage

May You remember what happened the first time Harry called at our house?
Annie Even if I can remember you'll still tell me.
May Mi dad was in the bath, he'd just come in from After's. Harry was waiting outside the front door. When he knocked on the door mi dad opened the bathroom window, saw who it was, and threw a bucket a' mucky bath water all over him.
Annie Why?
May He hated Harry, because he came from Upton.
Annie Well, it is three miles away.
May I'd known him a year even then.
Annie What, before you brought him home?
May Yeh.
Annie Bloody hell.
May We didn't do a lot that night.
Annie No?
May No, we stayed in and sat by the fire until he dried off. He's got a weak chest, you know? Nearly caught his death.
Annie Mi dad's a bugger.
May We'd been courting about eighteen month, and I think somebody must have told him at t' pit that I was seeing Harry, and that we were going to the pictures. So ... anyway we come out of the pictures and who's there waiting for me?
Annie Mi dad ...
May I could have bloody died.
Annie They get on now though, don't they?
May Oh yeh.
Annie Thought so.
May But they don't talk.
Annie That's probably why they get on.
May If mi dad strung a sentence together he'd bloody choke hissen.
Annie I think he likes Roy.
May Yeh, I think he does.
Annie (*to the audience*) During the early fifties the four of us went everywhere together.
May We were one big family.

The Lights change. The mirror-ball is struck

> *Roy and Harry enter with picnic gear, they are dressed in suits in the height of fashion*

Roy Every weekend we got on a bus and got away from it all.
Annie Harry would try his hand at singing.

Harry sings a few lines of "Hold Me, Hold Me"

May And Roy would tell awful jokes . . .

Roy Right, there's these two nuns.

Harry ⎱
May ⎰ *(together)* We've heard it.

Annie And we went dancing to the Palais de Dance at Hemsworth, Tassels at Royston.

May The Astoria at Goldthorpe.

Annie We went on mystery trips.

Roy Where the bloody hell are we?

Annie Club trips to Cleethorpes. Racing at Doncaster. We had picnics in Pontefract Castle, and these two went swimming in Ponte Park . . . it seemed to me that every day was a holiday.

They sit together. Silence

Roy I don't think we're going to have any kids for a few years.

Harry Why, don't you know what to do?

Roy Why, what do you do?

May If you don't know, Roy, I'm not tellin' you.

Annie I'll tell you after, love.

Roy Yeh . . . I'm a bit slow when it comes to things like that. Don't the storks still bring 'em?

Annie Roy says we should wait a bit.

Roy I'm gunna get out of the pit, Harry. Get involved in a sat down job, make a fortune, and come back and live in a big house. And then you two . . .

May When we're old and wizen'd . . .

Roy You two'll say, "they bloody did it".

Annie We'll have a big house.

Roy Oh ay, we'll have a big house, we'll be known as the folks who live on the hill . . .

Annie And then after the first million, then we'll have kids.

Harry Bloody hell, you'll be rusty by then.

May I think I want a son.

Roy Oh bloody hell, look out, Harry.

Harry You don't want it now, do you?

May Why?

Harry I've got a headache . . .

Annie Oh you silly sod . . .

Laughter

A bloody headache?

May No, I want a son, an' he'll be a big strapping lad, like mi dad.

Harry And he'll work with me down t'pit . . . So as I shall seh, nip up there, kid, and bring me some sandwiches, be a good lad.

May He'll not go down t'pit. He'll work in a bank.

Harry He could work in Roy's business.

Annie That's a good idea, we could make it a family affair, like McAlpine's. I'll be Roy's secretary, Harry can be one of the workmen.

Harry A scrubber?

Annie Yeh a scrubber, Harry, yeh ... And our May can make the tea ...

May Bloody typical that is and all.

Roy Roy and Annie married in nineteen fifty-four, true to Roy's cavalier fashion they honeymooned in France. They had four days in Paris.

Annie Mi dad was ill for three days when I got married. He cried all through the ceremony and all through the reception.

Roy They bought a house in Kirkby, after all, it was an investment.

Annie Roy was very handy about the house, he would put up shelves, decorate and keep the garden tidy. He built a rockery, and painted two little gnomes and even made a bird-bath.

Roy I might build a fish-pond.

Annie A fish-pond? What for?

Roy To put bloody fish in.

Annie Don't be daft, we don't want a fish. Nobody in Kirkby has a fish pond.

Roy We will. It'll put value on the house.

Annie But next-door's cats might eat the fish.

Roy and Annie exit with the picnic gear

May May and Harry were married in nineteen fifty-five. They had waited till after Christmas so they were in a new tax year, and with the tax they both got back, Harry bought a new car ... I wanted to buy a house ...

Harry Ha ha ha, a new car ... best car down Clayton Street.

May So we moved into a rented pithouse. The move to Upton upset mi dad; he seemed to be morose all the time, now me and our Annie had left home. He was completely alone.

Harry He'll manage, he can visit when he likes.

May I felt a great sense of freedom; living in my own house.

Harry We had a new car at the garden gate.

May And an enormous gramophone-cum-wireless.

Harry It was all we needed.

Time has passed. Music: "Begin the Beguine". *May and Harry dance*

Roy and Annie come on, carrying chairs. Annie is very elated

Annie Oh my God ... Oh my God ... I don't believe it.

May Settle down ...

Annie screams

Annie? You're delirious.

Annie What'll mi dad say? I'm going to be an aunty. Bloody hell, Roy, I'm going to be an aunty, what do you reckon?

Roy I didn't know you had it in you.

May I can't believe it ... I just can't.

Harry I know I look a bit slow, Roy, but I know how many beans mek five.

Annie When's it due?

May It?

Annie Well ... you know what I mean.

May February.

Roy Well, I suppose congratulations are in bloody order. Well done, May love ... smashing, I'm proud of you.

Roy leans and kisses May

May Thanks, Roy.

Roy Well done, you bugger ...

Harry She's the bloody hero, Roy, she's got to go through all the agony.

Annie You're so cheerful.

Roy Uncle Roy! Bloody hell, I feel like I've just been knighted ... Hey, we want to take him out you know, when he's here.

Annie He? Might be a she.

Roy Might be.

Harry What about two?

Roy We're waiting to see what happens. If this newsagent's shop in Wetherby comes off, we'll be up and off.

Harry You want to be careful, you know, Roy. I knew a bloke who once bought a paper shop ...

Roy Ay, and it blew away, I know it.

May We've got a lot of things to do in the house before I have it. And he's next to bloody hopeless with his hands. When we first got married he couldn't make a cuppa tea.

Harry I can boil an egg.

May He's the only fella I know who actually burns water.

Harry Any chance she gets to have a dig at me, Roy, she will do.

May I'll tell you what he does.

Harry Oh spare us.

May No ... I want our Annie to hear this. He comes home from the pit, and he's that bloody tired, and such an idle sod, he goes to sleep on the kitchen floor in his pit-muck.

Harry Once, I've done that, once.

May More than bloody once.

Annie You don't want to be letting her do all the fetching and carrying now, Harry.

Harry I don't do, Annie.

May He bloody will.

Harry I won't.

May I have to do the bloody garden.

Annie Can't Harry do it?

Harry I get hay-fever.

Annie Make sure she's all right, you know?

Harry I will.

Roy Course he will, bloody hell, you always look on the black side.

Harry I'm going to make sure everything's perfect for her, aren't I?

May I want some bloody new lino going down in that back passage.

Harry I'll see to it, leave it to me. I'm not kidding, Annie, your May is house mad.

Annie You shouldn't let her over-do it.
Harry I won't.
May He's not a bad old foul pig of a fella.
Roy She loves him to bloody death.
May He's a worm, Roy, but I love him . . .

Music: "Elmer's Tune". *Harry walks to a spotlight downstage* c

May exits

Roy and Annie remain frozen

Harry (*to the audience*) In nineteen fifty-six May gave birth to a big baby
boy. He was born at Southmoor Hospital, Hemsworth, and weighed ten
pounds at birth. May was severely ill, she was in a coma for twenty-four
hours, had a blood transfusion, and didn't see her son till a full four days
later. When she did see the baby, her eyes lit up, and she smiled a smile so
wide that I thought her face would split in two. She was so proud, so full
of happiness and warmth and for the first time in our lives, I think we
understood the meaning of the word love.

Black-out

Harry exits

Roy and Annie come to life. The Lights come up

Roy I never looked at Betty Lewis.
Annie I saw you looking at her at the dance.
Roy I never was!
Annie You were I saw you, every time she passed our table you couldn't
stop yourself from having a look at her.
Roy All right, all right, I was looking at her, can't I bloody look at another
woman now, can't I even speak to another woman?
Annie It was the way you were looking.
Roy What am I supposed to do if I go into a bloody shop and a nice woman
comes to serve me? What am I supposed to do, ask for a bloke to serve
me. For God's sake grow up, or get bloody lost.
Annie I can't help being me, Roy.
Roy I know that . . . bloody hell, I know that much.
Annie Do you think I want to be like this? Do you think I want to be upset
all the time? Do you think I don't want to have kids?
Roy Leave it now, let's not start all that again.
Annie How do you think I feel inside?
Roy I know how you feel, Annie, I feel the same myself. Forget it now.
Annie I can't just forget it.
Roy It's not your fault, is it? Nobody's blaming you. Don't take it out on
yourself.
Annie Our May was the one who was always ill as a kid, and she's OK . . . I
can't understand it.
Roy Leave it now . . .
Annie But I want kids, Roy, I want 'em.

Roy I know you do. I was the one who said we'd wait.

Annie I feel so empty inside. I feel like my whole inside is rotting away. I wish I could rip my stomach out.

Roy Stop getting worked up, Annie, stop it! We've been over this a million times; we've seen every bloody specialist in the area. There's no chance, listen to me, no chance. So that's it. It's over, forget it. Let us please just get on with our lives ...

Annie Don't tell our May.

Roy Why am I going to tell your May? What am I going to do, run round and tell her?

Annie I don't want anybody to know.

Roy Nobody will. Now bloody calm down. It's not the end of the world. We've got each other, bloody hell, we've got each other.

Annie I wish I could start my life all over again, Roy. I wish I could wipe the slate clean. Start afresh.

Roy When we get this paper shop in Wetherby it'll be a whole new life for us.

Annie I feel like I've let you down.

Roy Don't be daft.

Annie I love you, Roy ... I don't think I could live without you.

The Lights fade to deep blue. Music: Dick Haymes "You'll Never Know"

Roy and Annie dance off. May enters. She wears a headscarf and is pushing a pram. She stands in a spotlight

May Mi dad was over the moon when he saw the baby, he didn't say much to Harry, just told him to look after me, and then he started to cry. We took him down to mi dad's regular. Mi dad would just stand with the pram looking at him, never saying a word. Then one day I overheard him saying, "I'm thee grandad". On Sunday afternoons our Annie would take him up on to the common.

The Lights change. It is 1957

Annie enters and takes the pram from May who exits. Mrs Gillespie enters

Annie pushes the pram DR, *Mrs Gillespie follows her*

Mrs Gillespie Oh he's smashing, int he?

Annie Yeh.

Mrs Gillespie He's lovely, aren't you? How old is he?

Annie Thirteen months.

Mrs Gillespie Oh he's smashing.

Annie Yeh, it's a bit cold to have him out though.

Mrs Gillespie It'll blow the cobwebs off him. Yeh?

Annie Yeh.

Mrs Gillespie You'll be glad to have got him out of the way. That's what I thought when I had my first. Get the first one out of the way and then you're laughing. I mean look at mi daughter. Twenty last week and she's had a little girl, oh she's smashing and all, cheeky little face she's got. I

wanted to call her Kathleen, but they've christened her Kay ... Oh look
at him, he's smashing. She's got the first one out of the way ...

Annie First? Yeh.

Mrs Gillespie You take my word for it, love. The first is always the worst.
Oh, but he is lovely, he is. Look here's sixpence for him.

Annie Oh thanks.

Mrs Gillespie How's your dad?

Annie You know, getting by.

Mrs Gillespie Your May married yet?

Annie Yeh, married, lives in Upton.

Mrs Gillespie Oh ... Has she had any?

Annie No ... no not yet ...

Mrs Gillespie Well, there's time for her, int there?

Annie Yeh.

Mrs Gillespie But he's smashing he is, aren't you?

Annie The nurse said I'd got to bring him back when he was twenty-one.

Mrs Gillespie I should think so and all. He's bloody smashing.

Mrs Gillespie leaves. Roy appears

Roy and Annie look into the pram

Annie Don't wake him, Roy.

Roy I'm not doing ...

Annie You are ...

Roy I'm not ... (*Singing*) "Hush-a-bye baby on the tree top, when the wind
blows the cradle will rock ..."

Annie What did they say?

Roy Three weeks.

Annie (*shouting*) Three.

Roy Sssshh. Three weeks, and we can move into the shop. We can get away
from Kirkby, I can get out of that shit-hole and we'll be living it up in
Wetherby ...

Annie And he'll be able to come and see us, won't you, eh? You'll have to
come and visit your Aunty Annie and Uncle Roy, in their big new house
in Wetherby ...

Roy You'll like that, won't you? Eh? We'll have a swing, and your Uncle
Roy'll make a tree-house.

Annie I want to adopt, Roy.

Roy I know.

Annie I do.

Roy I know you do.

Annie Promise we can.

Roy Yes.

Annie Promise.

Roy Promise. Cross my heart hope to die.

Annie I can't believe that it's all happening like we planned.

Roy Well it is ...

Annie Well, kiss me then.

Roy I'll kiss you after.

Annie Kiss me now.

He does so

> See that, Paul, did you see that? Your uncle Roy kissed me then. Mmmmmm. (*To the baby*) Mmmmmm. Shall we go to the dance tonight?

Roy If you want to go to the dance, we'll go to the dance.

Annie Shall we take you back to your mam, shall we?

The Lights change. Music: Bing Crosby's "Piociana". Roy and Annie leave the pram and go UL and dance in a spotlight. A wind machine howls

> *May enters and stands C in a spotlight. Harry enters in mining gear and moves into a spotlight DR*

Harry We were working in the new face, three's face, very low, very warm, no room to move, like being in a bath of dust, more room in a tub, couldn't turn around, blackness and noise all about, and the beams of light sent shadows all over your world. Your world was two feet nine high, black, grit black, shiny black coal. Me and Roy are working; it's snap time, I tell him that I'm going up to Three's Junction snap there, it's cooler, more room. And we're snapping, and I have to drop mi pants, there's no shit-house down there, and Roy says "go as far away as you can, I've got luncheon meat on my bread". So I did. I walk for five minutes up through Three's Heading just to drop mi pants. And Roy was sat there chuntering to hissen, sat alone, eating luncheon meat. (*Quick pause*) And the roof went, a junction girder collapsed, letting the junction in; a large steel, strong ... girder collapsed. Two hundred tonnes of stone came crashing in.

Mr Poole (*off*) There's an accident in Three's Junction.

Harry Two hundred tonnes of stone came crashing down pinning him to the floor, nailing him to the dust. The noise was deafening. *Roy!*

Annie Roy!

Roy stops dancing and exits

May Roy!

Harry *Roy.*

Mr Poole (*off*) Get some men down there.

Harry Dust, like fog, dust so thick it clogged up your every pore, settled in your lungs like sand in an hour-glass. Roy! We managed to get him out, twelve men dug him out. A doctor administered morphia. He was alive when they brought him out of the pit. I told Annie, "Don't worry, love, he's alive, he was alive when they brought him out of the pit." He was alive when they brought him out of the pit—that's what they said ... But how could he be? He was crushed to death, crushed to a wafer. He died on the way to the hospital. I felt so sorry for Roy, but I felt even more sense of sorrow for those he's left behind.

A howling wind is heard

> *Harry slowly turns and leads May and his son in the pram off*

Annie stands alone, C, lit by one spotlight. The wind blows. She is in utter grief

Annie Oh God . . . oh God . . . Oh my God . . . HELP ME . . . HELP ME . . . Roy . . . Oh God . . . Roy . . . Roy . . . I wish the earth would burn up. I wish every piece of coal in the earth would burn up . . . every rotting coffin catch light. I wish every miner was dead . . . I do, that's what I wish . . . I wish every miner was dead . . . Roy, Roy, ROY, ROY!

Music: Bob Hope's "Thanks for the Memory" *and fades slowly. Meanwhile, the Lights change*

   Mrs Potter, May's neighbour, is frozen in a spotlight upstage. Annie exits

When the music has gone, Mrs Potter, with a lighted cigarette, steams downstage to call her son in. The Lights change

Mrs Potter Ian . . . Ian? Get in this bleeding house now.

   May enters with a brush, sweeping up the soil which has been thrown by the neighbours

May Look at the soddin' mess.
Mrs Potter Come on here, I shalln't say it agen.
May I'm not having it, you know, love.
Mrs Potter Not having what?
May All this soil on my path.
Mrs Potter There's only two pieces!
May I'm not bothered. I've had to sweep it up twice already.
Mrs Potter Get in this bleeding house now!
May You can't control your kids.
Mrs Potter Come on here.
May That young 'un of yours is going to catch its death. He's running about with no shoes and socks on, bare-arsed.
Mrs Potter That's my bloody business.
May I don't want 'em throwing soil on my path, not when I'm trying to keep my house tidy . . . And you could do with some soap and water round your house, instead of going to the club every bloody dinner-time . . .
Mrs Potter Don't waste your bloody breath. If you want to kill yoursen cleaning up all the bloody time, bully for you . . .
May You little worm, I'll break your bloody nose . . .
Mrs Potter Oh pull the other one, Mrs Hickman, it's got pissing bells on . . . Come on here . . . now!

   Mrs Potter exits. Harry, tired and moody, returns home. The Lights change

May Late.
Harry Am I?
May Wondered where you were?
Harry Cemetery.
May Tea's ready.
Harry Don't want any.
May Don't have it then.

Harry I just called to see him, first time since, nice head-stone. Don't reckon much to the verse.

May Our Annie picked it.

Harry Typical.

May Tea's on. Be stewed by now. All settlemented.

Harry I heard you the first time.

May Only saying.

Harry Only saying? You're getting on my bloody nerves with it.

May You're getting on mine.

Harry Am I?

May They're a bloody nuisance them next door. She can't control them kids. If our Paul turns out like them I'll kill him.

Harry Where is he?

May Int room . . . Now get your tea.

Harry Where's the butter on this bread?

May Why?

Harry Where's the butter?

May On the bread.

Harry I don't call that butter, I like a lot of butter, not just a wipe.

May Get it eaten.

Harry Call that butter?

May What do you call it, shit?

Harry I want a lot of butter when you butter my bread.

May Do it your bloody self next time. You never do anything in this bloody house. You're useless.

Harry You're the woman . . . I bring the money in. You do everything in this house. Or do you want to swap jobs, and go down that shit-hole every day.

May You never do a bloody thing, you don't.

Harry You silly woman.

May Stop shouting.

Harry I'll swing for you. This is my house, I pay the rent here and I want more butter on my bread, do you hear me?

May You'll get it on, you'll get it . . . I'll put that much on next time, it'll bloody choke you to death.

Harry Go on shout, you daft sod, that's all you bloody do.

May You're the one who's shouting, not me. You're the one who brings unpleasantness into this house, you, not me.

Harry You must be joking, every time I come home you've got a face as long as a wet week. I can't help it if you can't get on with the neighbours. You're like your father, unsociable, you can't talk to people.

May Why don't you shut your silly bloody mouth? Go to bed, you're that tired you don't know what you're saying.

The Lights change. Music: Nat King Cole "When I Fall in Love". May and Harry freeze

Annie enters. She looks older and drawn

Annie (*to the audience*) There were no arguments in my house, everything was still and quiet. And even in nineteen sixty-five, despite Elvis n' Gene Pitney, I still cried for Roy. I had tried to meet another man at the Welfare Dance, but I'm not that sort of person. I was coping by myself. Just.

Harry But in nineteen sixty-six tragedy struck the Parker sisters. Big John Parker their father died of a heart attack.

Annie He was buried next to mi mam, and was, we all hoped, the last Parker to lose his life for coal.

May Mi dad had had pneumoconiosis for years, but the doctor insisted that that wasn't the cause of death.

Harry May was shattered when her father died, she became even more neurotic, and the smile that she often smiled in her youth was seldom ever seen.

Annie During this time Harry had a number of minor accidents at the pit. He'd lost two toes off his left foot.

Harry And I had the top of my thumb taken off, but it was nothing to get excited about, and I could still dance.

May If anything he was all the more nibbler.

Annie May poured all her interests into Paul—he couldn't trump in public without his mother knew about it.

The Lights change

Annie and Harry exit

May turns to the audience

May (*shouting*) Paul? Paul?

Paul answers, off, then enters. He is ten years of age, with big ears. He wears short pants. Tosh, the same age, is also in tow

Paul Paul Hickman was an only child, and in nineteen sixty-six he was a ten-year-old marble champion. Having just beaten his best friend Tosh for six large bollies. He was the best marble player in Upton.

May Come on, it's half-six.

Paul Can't I stay out? Tosh is.

Tosh Mi mam lets me stay out till eight.

May No, come on, your dad'll be home soon.

Paul Oh Mam, we've got another championship to play.

May Well you'll have to play it tomorra, I want you in the bath.

Paul Why do I allus have to come in early?

May 'Cos you do, I've got my routine. Tosh can stay out because his mam washes the little 'uns first.

Paul But, Mam?

May I want you in, now. The more sleep you have the more intelligent you'll be when you grow up. Now come on, I've got some boiled fish for your supper. Fish for brains my mam used t'say.

Tosh See you tomorra. Play a twenty-niner ...

May Paul, come on, now!

May exits

Kay Cooper, aged ten, suddenly arrives on stage

Paul and Tosh look at her

Kay Are you playing marbles?
Tosh No, he's got to go in.
Kay Why?
Tosh His mam ses.
Kay I can stop out. Mi mam ses I can stay out till nine o'clock.
Tosh Nine o'clock?
Kay Yeh. Are you playing then? I've got some bollies.
Tosh Play a twenty-niner?
Kay Yeh ... mi name's Kay ... come on ...
Tosh Are you coming?
Paul Can't. Mi mam'll hit me.
Tosh I'll see you.
Paul She's a lass ...
Tosh I know. See you.
Paul Zig.
Tosh Zog ...

Tosh leaves with Kay

Paul watches them go. Music: "Begin the Beguine"

Paul (*to the audience*) I don't think I'll ever forget those years ... I failed my eleven-plus, and I didn't get a racing bike: I got a good hiding instead. I think mi mam n' dad were embarrassed because I'd failed. Most other kids in our class had passed. But I wasn't really bothered. What I resented most though in nineteen sixty-seven was having to go to bed when it was still light outside, I would lay awake and listen to Tosh and the other kids playing French Cricket or Best-Man-Falls ... and downstairs I could hear mi mam n' dad dancing to old time records ...

Music: a slow foxtrot

Harry and May enter dancing

May We were the best dancers at the Welfare.
Harry Slow, slow, quick quick, slow.
Paul (*to the audience*) Mi man said that going to bed early would make me intelligent, but I had my doubts about that. During this time mi dad used to pinch my nose and pretend that he had it in his hand, and he was forever showing me a trick where his thumb seemed to split into two pieces ... I was beginning to think that it was mi dad who should go to bed early.

Paul exits

May and Harry still dance, then they drift apart

Harry Come on ...

May No . . .

Harry Yes.

May I can't cope with another one, not at my age.

Harry All you had to do was have him, I washed all the nappies, I did all the shitty work.

May I'm not arguing about it, I'm not having another kid and that's that . . .

Harry I bloody hate you sometimes.

May Ay and I hate you.

Harry Well tek off then, sling your hook.

May Shurrup shouting this time of night.

Harry I shall shout if I want, it's my house.

May Go on then, shout, you're like a big soft kid, shouting because he can't have his own way. Banging bloody doors and shouting . . .

Paul enters dressed in his pyjamas

Paul What's up, Mam?

May Nowt, go back to bed.

Harry Paul, tell your mother that she's a foul pig of a woman.

May And tell your dad he can shit.

Harry Tell her that I'm going to Sheffield and I'm not coming back.

May Tell him: good.

Harry Tell her, I mean it.

May Tell him, he can do what the bloody hell he likes. In fact, you can tell him that I'll leave, I'll go down to our Annie's, she's fed up of being by herself. He can have all the bloody house work, see how he likes it.

Harry Tell her, she's got a bloody screw loose.

May Tell him, it's him who's got the screw loose, all their families alike, they're all bloody barmy.

Paul slowly turns and walks off stage. Annie enters during the following

Harry At least my family bloody talk. You father never spoke two words to me.

May What about your father, he didn't know what work was.

Harry At least he was bloody sociable. Your father was a bad pig he treated your mother like shit.

May Don't you talk about my family, you.

Harry You're all bloody barmy.

May Go on, tek off, go on, go . . . I don't ever want to see you again.

Harry I'm going, don't worry.

May I don't know where you're going, nobody's daft enough to bloody have you.

Harry Do you honestly think you'd be able to get rid of me that easy, you foul swine?

May No, I don't. Worse luck.

Annie In nineteen seventy, as a break from the boredom of home, I went away for a few days with our May and Harry. They didn't argue much. We went to Blackpool. We took our Paul, and trailed him around the shops, poor sod. Then I dragged him around the tower ballroom. I'm sure our Paul is the clumsiest sod who ever walked a pair of shoes.

Harry Pit life continued very much the same, except that Mr Poole the under-manager had been killed, and I was working in a face that had two inches of water. The NCB had opened a new social centre which suited me and May, it was just right for dancing.

May I had my kitchen sink moved into the passage, a lot of folk were having it done, and we were thinking of buying a fridge. Jean Clayworth had got one so I thought it only fair that I should have one. Our Paul seemed to be happy; they said he was above average at his new school.

May, Annie and Harry exit

Kay, now fourteen years old, runs on stage, followed by Paul also fourteen

Kay Catch us then? . . . If you want it . . .
Paul When I do Kay, I'm gunna get you.
Kay Gis a kiss then. Come here . . .
Paul What?
Kay Yeh . . . there's nobody about.

They force their lips together, a lot of noise

Paul Hang on you're breaking my teeth, you're pushing too hard.
Kay Have I got soft lips?
Paul Yeh.
Kay Shall I open my mouth?
Paul What for?
Kay French kissing it's called.
Paul If you want . . .

They kiss, it is sloppy and wet, still very noisy

   Hang, on, I'm getting wet all over . . .
Kay Feel me . . .
Paul Oh God . . .
Kay Come on, Paul, feel me . . .

Paul begins to feel Kay, about her legs and ribs. A tango is performed. Paul speaks through it

Paul (*to the audience*) Me and Kay were in the same class at school. There was something about Kay. Every time I got close to her I felt excited . . . every time I was near her, I couldn't leave her alone.

Paul tries to undo her bra through her jumper

Kay What're you doing?
Paul Nowt.
Kay You're squashing me . . . Paul, I can't breathe. I get asthma, Paul . . . What're you trying to do?
Paul No . . . missed it . . . hang on.
Kay Do you want me to do it?

Paul No, hang about, I'll do it.
Kay Hurry up.
Paul Oh shit, I'm gerrin cramp in my leg. Oh shit. Bloody hell.
Kay This is very romantic, I can't breathe, you know?
Paul Nearly, hang on. Turn around.
Kay Why?
Paul Done it.
Kay Now what are you gunna do?

Kay runs off

Paul is left. The Lights change

His mother and father, with Aunty Annie, enter

It is in every way a domestic scene. Annie is in washing-up gloves, Harry sits reading a newspaper

May I want a word with you, mi lad.
Paul What's up?
Harry Your mother's got a bee in her bonnet.
May I'll tell you what's up. I thought you said that that mark on your neck was a bruise?
Paul What mark?
Annie Leave him, May.
May No, Annie, I want to get to the bottom of this.
Harry She'll have her way, Annie.
Annie He's only doing what's natural.
Harry She'll drive that lad away from us. You mark my words.
May Shut up, you!
Harry Bloody hell.
May Why didn't you tell us you had a girl-friend?
Paul Well ...
May Are you hiding things from us now. You've been a different lad since you've been to that school.
Paul No, Mam ...
Annie Let him be, May. Look at him, poor sod, he's sweating.
May What are you doing letting somebody give you a love bite on your neck. Are you thick?
Paul No, Mam.
May You bloody are.
Harry Leave him now ...
May I never let your father do that sort of thing to me. Who is she ... ?
Paul Who?
May You know bloody well who.
Paul Just a lass.
May I want to know who she is ...
Annie Give it a miss, May, bloody hell.
Paul Kay.
May Kay what?
Paul Cooper, she lives down the other end.

May Right I'm going to see her mam and dad and tell her to stop seeing you.

Paul Mam!

Harry This bloody family.

Annie Poor lad's scared to death.

Paul I don't love her, Mam ...

May You listen to me.

Harry She'll not give up, she'll not bloody give up until he's crying ...

Paul Honest, Mam, I don't love her, I never said I did. I'm shakin', I'm scared, Mam ... Look at me ...

May You make your mind up, it's me or her, you make your mind up, Paul, because if you see her again, I'm going, I'm off ... I'm going to pack my bloody bags and go ...

Paul (*crying*) Mam ...

May Stop crying, stop it, you're fifteen, now stop it ...

Annie Calm down, bloody hell calm down ...

Harry I could bloody belt you for doing that to him, I could ...

May I bloody love him ...

Annie Well show it ...

Paul (*crying*) Aunty Annie ...

Annie You're bloody setting me off, look at what you're doing. I'm bloody glad that I never had any kids ... I bloody am.

Tosh, dressed in seventies' school uniform enters US *and watches the scene before speaking. May and Annie exit*

Tosh Is thy having a game of table tennis?

Paul No I'm stopping in.

Tosh Oh I'll go play by myself then.

Tosh exits

Music plays: "Volare" *then fades slowly. Paul uses the beat of the music to address the audience*

Paul I never told mi mam but I was still seeing Kay, all the way through mi exams. And I never told Kay the way mi mam was with girls. I don't know what it was but during this time I began to realize that I was going to die, I would lay awake thinking about my own death, and how unfair it was because the world would continue ... I don't want to die, Dad.

Harry What?

Paul I don't want to die.

Harry Neither do I.

Harry exits

Paul The only thing that made me feel good about dying was that Mark Thompson, the cock of the school would have to die as well.

The Lights change

Kay enters wearing clothes she would on her way back from a chocolate factory

Kay I'm here, Paul . . .

Paul Kay had left school and had got a job at the chocolate factory. Kay was one of the few things that kept my mind off dying. I would lay in bed at nights and imagine that we were naked together, or imagine that I was rubbing my face between her breasts. Sometimes I even imagined that we were married and had little kids. I wanted to be with Kay forever.

Kay Are you coming to the Youth Club?

Paul Dunno.

Kay I don't know why I bother going out with you. You're pathetic, you can never come out.

Paul I can. I can do what I want.

Kay You can't, you're tied to t' apron strings.

Paul I'm not. Kiss me.

Kay Is that all you can say? You should leave school, Paul, and come out into the real world. It's brill, I can do what I want. I want a man, you know Paul, not a shirt button.

Paul I've got mi exams, ant I?

Kay I might finish with you!

Paul Don't. Kiss me.

Kay For somebody who's supposed to be brainy you're crap with words, aren't you?

Paul We don't talk to each other in our house, Kay, we just grunt at each other and point like chimps. We don't need words in our house.

Kay What's gunna happen if you go to college?

Paul Nowt . . . Kiss us, Kay . . .

Kay No . . . not here. You sex maniac. I will if you come to the Youthy.

Paul I can't. Mi homework.

Kay There isn't such a word as "can't". Some lasses at work have been telling me about having it off. They say it's great. Best feeling in the world.

Paul Rather have a laugh, you can have a laugh in Woolies.

Kay They say you should've done it by sixteen. I told 'em about you. I said he's got eight O levels, they said well he should know what to do. Do you wanna do it?

Paul Kiss us . . .

Kay We could do it tonight. Gerrin excited?

Paul Yeh . . .

Kay Do you wanna do it, have it off?

Paul You're too nice . . . just kiss us.

Kay Don't you want it?

Paul cannot bear it. Music plays: Elvis's "Fever". Kay flaunts. They dance. Out of the night is the voice of Aunty Annie, sounding like Mother

Annie (*off*) Paul?

Paul Shit . . . mi mam.

   Annie enters

Annie Hey up, kid!

Paul Oh hey up, Aunty Annie, I thought it was mi mam.

Annie What you up to then, you bugger?

Paul Nowt, just talking. This is Kay, Aunty Annie. Mi girl-friend . . . I told you about her.

Annie I know yu' grandma, don't I? Lives just down the road from me. Work at Terry's, don't you? Chocolate factory?

Kay Yeh, for about six months.

Annie I used t'work there, mind you it was Blakey's then—seg factory. Eeee, I love them chocolate oranges. Do you make 'em. I love them. Couldn't get us some, could you? I could do with some of them, eh Paul?

Kay Anyway . . . I'll get off. Might see you down the Youthy later. If you can come down. I'll bring mi chocolate oranges for you to look at. Tara.

Kay leaves

Paul and Annie watch her go

Annie That's who all the palaver's over, is it?

Paul Don't tell mi mam, will you?

Annie You little bugger.

Paul Don't tell mi mam, Aunty Annie, will you?

Annie No . . . I can keep a secret, kid. I'm good at keeping secrets. Been doing it all my life. You go and enjoy yoursen, eh? Bloody hell . . .

Paul Gi up Aunty Annie, I'm going red.

Annie She's a big strapping lass. You go and enjoy yourself while you can. Before old age creeps up on you, and you seize up. I wish I was sixteen and knew what I know now, I do. Go and fly your kite before your nerves get bad like mine. I'm on three different coloured tablets now. Mi nerves are shocking. I won't tell your mam, I promise. I can keep a secret.

Annie exits

Paul (*to the audience*) Mi Aunty Annie kept saying her nerves were bad, I should think they were, creeping about like that. She was like a bloody ghost, she drifted about everywhere. Her nerves were bad. At least she lived on her own; she should come and try living in the asylum I laughingly call home. Living in our house was turning me into a nervous wreck.

Black-out

Paul exits

Smoke fills the stage. Music plays: "Ziggy Stardust". *The Lights come up*

Tosh, in full face make up, enters playing a sweeping brush. Paul appears, carrying an album cover, a sketch and a tennis racquet

Paul puts the album cover on a chair and mimes to the music with the tennis racquet

Harry and May enter and watch in silence

Harry Bloody hell!

May What are you two up to?

Paul Well, just nowt really.

Harry You're bloody slack the pair on you. What's tha supposed to be, Tosh?

Tosh Ziggy Stardust and the Spiders from Mars.

May Does your mam know about this?

Tosh No, she dun't like Bowie.

Harry I'm slogging my knackers off at pit . . .

May Language!

Harry And there's two blokes as big as hosses acting goat miming to records. You're bloody sick. I thought tha wa' supposed to be revising?

Paul I am.

Harry What we got a bloody Martian here for then?

Tosh Just beamed down to get some history books.

Harry Come on, get t' kettle on, mek us a drink.

Paul I'm doing sommat.

May Kettle on . . . now.

Paul Or . . . doing sommat . . .

Tosh I'll have to get off then.

Harry Ar, go and plague somebody else.

Tosh Nice to see you, Mr Hickman. Nice to see Earthlings. I'll get off. I've got another planet to visit. Zig.

Tosh leaves

May picks up a sketch done by Paul

Paul Zog.

May What's this, our Paul? "Sex creatures from the planet Creedos"?

Paul A level Art, Mam.

Harry I bloody wonder about thee.

May I don't understand it.

Harry Tha like a bloody woman. Why don't you get out and get some fresh air. Thy hasn't been wearing make up, has tha?

Paul No . . . just Tosh . . . He's a laugh, int he.

Harry Ay, bloody hilarious.

Paul (*to the audience*) I don't think mi dad appreciated our sense of humour. In fact, I don't know where my humour came from, everybody in our house was always at each other's throats.

Paul and Harry exit. Annie enters, very distraught

Annie I can't cope wi' it, May . . . Not any longer I just can't.

May What's happened?

Annie That house, it's coming in on me. I can't stay by myself any longer, kid, I'll have to have some company, it's sending me round the twist.

Paul enters. He is eighteen now

Paul Sup——

Annie I don't want to upset you, I can't stay there . . . I've got to stop somewhere else, May, I've just got to.

May You can stop wi' us, stop int spare room.

Paul Brilliant idea that, Mother, where am I gunna revise? We can't swing a cat in this house.

Annie I don't want to put our Paul off his work, I'll nip down to Roy's mam's; she might be able to see to me.

May You're stopping here.

Annie If he's got exams, it's his future.

May You're stopping here. His dad'll have sommat to say to him, he's not too big to get a clout.

Paul Sorry, Aunty Annie. I blurted something out, first thing that came into mi head.

May You always do.

Paul I wonder who I tek after? Sorry, Aunty Annie.

Annie S'all right, kid.

May It allus happens to this family.

Paul Oh God, she's off now ...

May It allus happens.

Paul Jesus.

Annie Don't go upsetting yourself.

May I can't help it, everything happens to us. Look at that bloody lot next door, they don't work, four kids, the house is a mess, and all the heartache lands on our doorstep. (*In tears*) It's not bloody fair.

Paul I'm off out ...

Paul leaves

Annie comforts May

Annie Hey come on, you're a Parker, aren't you? Don't get upset. Hey, chin up! Happy birthday.

May Oh Annie, you don't know the half of it. I'm worrying myself to death.

Annie What about?

May I'm having such an awful time each month. Harry doesn't know, I've been to the doctor's. He's told me that it's my age. But ... I mean that's how mi mam started.

Annie See a specialist ... go private.

May I don't like. I don't want our Paul to know I'm not well. He went for an interview to Lancaster and he didn't get in. He's waiting to hear from Sussex now ... I hope to God he gets in.

Annie That's a long way off.

May He's set his heart and soul on it. I don't want to upset him, but I had to tell somebody, Annie, it's worrying me to death.

Music: "Moonlight Cocktail". *The Lights change*

Paul enters and watches as Annie and May exit

The spotlight picks out Paul as he slowly walks DR

During the following, Annie, May and Harry stretch out two washing lines and begin hanging up washing—clothing, net curtains, sheets, pillow cases etc. They are only dimly lit

Paul Nineteen seventy-four was like the end of an era for me. Tosh had been kicked out of the sixth form, and then went completely barmy and got a job down the pit. He was working with mi dad, which pissed mi dad off. But he was only there for two weeks and they were on strike . . . which suited Tosh. We started having power cuts and I started getting A's for my English essays. We were doing *Sons and Lovers* so that was a doddle for me. Mi aunty Annie was still ghosting about at home, keeping my secret, and forcing me to play Monopoly with her by candle-light. And mi mam seemed under the weather but her and mi dad still argued and danced and threw food at each other so it couldn't be anything serious. And after six weeks the miners had beaten Ted Heath. Mi dad was over the moon and so was Tosh and mi mam, so was everybody. Yeh, nineteen seventy-four seemed like a good year to me.

May I do feel bloody funny.

Harry She's been washing all day, you can't tell her.

May I feel bloody awful.

Harry It'll kill her all this bloody cleaning.

May What else is there to do?

Annie It's non-stop washing in this house.

May I want putting in a bag and shaking up.

Paul It's true; mi mam washed everything. As soon as you took a shirt off your back mi mam'd wash it, scrub the collar and have it drying around the fire. She washed towels before they were used, and sheets when I had only slept in them twice. She washed lace curtains four times a week. And our underwear every day. In nineteen seventy-four, I was the cleanest sixth-form student in Europe.

Harry She'll end up wi' arthritis.

Annie She's always got her hands in water.

Harry She'll be bloody crippled when she gets older.

Annie Housework'll be here when she isn't.

Harry It'll get in her bloody bones.

Harry, Annie and May exit

Paul She was obsessed with washing, with cleaning, with the house. We got a new three-piece suite in October nineteen seventy-two, and I swear that she wouldn't let me and mi dad sit on it till February nineteen seventy-four. But for all her washing, and ironing, and shouting and bickering and bullying and cleaning and polishing and arguing . . . I loved her.

Paul exits

The Lights change. A wind blows very strongly, it is overcast and rain can be heard—it's throwing it down

May runs on anxiously. She has a plastic bucket for the washing

May Oh bloody hell, look at the bloody weather. Annie? Annie . . . (*She starts to take the washing in*) Annie . . . Annie!

Annie runs on

Annie Oh hell.

May No rest for the bloody wicked. They said it was gunna be fine.

Annie Where's our Paul?

May Gone to t' shops. He'll be bloody drenched.

Annie Look at it, it's like the end of the world.

May Get 'em off. Don't trail 'em across the floor.

Annie Shall I tell Mrs Potter next door?

May You'd better.

Annie (*shouting*) Mrs Potter? Mrs Potter?

May Where's Harry? (*Shouting*) Maggie?

Annie Usual place.

May He's always ont bloody toilet.

Annie I don't think she can hear me, next door. Maggie ... Hello! Mrs
    Potter?

May I'll never get these buggers dried today. (*She has her arms full of
    clothes*)

Harry comes out into the rain, pulling up his trousers. He is holding a letter

Where've you been?

Harry Got a letter for our Paul.

May passes him and exits with the washing and then returns

Annie is still taking the washing off the line

Annie Get some o' these brought in.

Harry It's from Sussex. Just come ...

May Don't get the shirts I'll get them, get the sheets ... Don't let 'em trail
    on the floor.

Paul enters with Tosh, they are both fairly wet

Paul Bloody hell. We're soaked.

May Help your dad.

Tosh Do you want me to do owt ... ? Stopped raining now.

Annie Bring me the peg-bag.

Tosh Abandon ship abandon ship, get the washing in ...

Harry He's bloody barmy, that lad ...

May I'm never gunna get finished today, I'll have t' dry these around the
    fire.

Harry Letter for you ...

May Don't open it here.

Paul Why?

May Can't you wait till you get inside ...

Paul I'm opening it.

Annie (*shouting next door*) Maggie ... Maggie? Is she bloody deaf next
    door?

May Our Annie's more bothered about them next bloody door. Let's get
    our stuff in, sod 'em.

Tosh has an armful of clothes

Tosh What shall I do wi' these?
May Don't crumble 'em up, you silly sod.

Paul has opened the letter, and is reacting to the news. He has been offered a place to read English at Sussex

Annie It's raining love, your washing's getting wet.
Harry That's a bloody understatement.
Paul I've got in. Two C's and a D. They've offered me. I've got in.
May Can't you leave that?
Harry He's got a place ...
Annie I've been shouting you for ages ...
Tosh Bloody hell, brain-box!
Harry University?
Paul I can't believe it.
Harry Bloody university?
Annie First Hickman to get to university.
Harry Look at me, I'm bloody crying.
Paul I am.
Tosh I am, and I'm not going.
Annie Oh, I'm so pleased for you ...
Harry I could bloody eat you ...
Annie I wish mi dad could have lived to see him.
May Don't set yourself off.
Annie I do wish he could ...
Paul Look at us, we're bloody three sheets t' wind, we're all soaked.
Tosh It's ruining my hair ...
Annie Eee, we're proud of you.
May Never mind all this palaver ... let's get the bloody washing in before we all get pneumonia. Harry put the kettle on, we'll have to celebrate. We'll have a tot of sherry. Tosh come on. Paul bring that line in.
Tosh Hey you can't talk to him like that now you know, he's gunna have letters after his name.
May I'll talk to him how I want, just because he's got in at university doesn't mean he can't help me with the washing. Now come here, bring that bloody line in ... Bloody university. Bloody hell.

Harry, Annie and Tosh exit, followed by May. As May goes, Kay enters, dressed to go out

Music plays low: "Face the Music and Dance"

Kay My eighteenth today, or have you forgot? You said you'd come to Tiffany's with me when I was eighteen. Remember? Try and make an effort, Paul, if you think anything about me make an effort ... It's been three years ... Come on, Paul!

May comes out of the house

May (*calling loudly*) Paul, come on, we all waiting for you!

Silence

May goes

Paul takes his time and looks at Kay, then slowly he starts to leave her

Paul runs inside to his house

Kay is left alone. The music plays as the Lights fade to—

BLACK-OUT

ACT II

It is six years later: 1980

The Lights come up on a bare stage. Music plays: "The Anniversary Waltz

*May and Harry are waltzing together and singing the lyrics to the song. The
are both fifty-one. Annie is also there. She is forty-nine, thin and rather bad.
worn*

Harry In nineteen eighty it was me and May's Silver Wedding Anniversar
We celebrated in style at the new Welfare Club.
May All our friends were there. We had a "bring your own buffet".
Harry Which meant that everyone brought their own buffet.
May They know that, you sarcastic pig.
Harry May had made some mince pies.
May And there was pie and peas.
Harry Benny Mills had brought some sausage rolls.
May Our Annie had made a trifle.
Harry And Audrey Clarke had made some vol au vents.
May She never made them, they were from Marks and Spencer's.
Annie My trifle was going down well.
May It was everybody's favourite.
Annie I should think it was, I put nearly a full bottle of sherry in it. Tosh ha
already had three helpings.
Harry Who invited that daft sod?
May There was Bingo.
Harry There bloody would be.
May And a spot waltz. It was smashing.
Harry It was just what we wanted, not too hectic. If I get excited it sets m
chest off.
May Our Paul had come home especially. Where is he?
Harry Who?
May Our Paul?
Harry Somewhere.
Annie He's enjoying hissen, he likes to come back up home.
May He'd done well at university. And he said that he came home when h
could.
Harry He'd got two degrees. Did his second one part-time.
May He didn't get a grant so I decided to give him the thousand pound
that mi dad'd left.
Harry We're proud of him.
May He get's all choked up talking about him.

Harry I'm proud of him.

May We've got his cap and gown photo on the mantelpiece.

Annie I had moved into a smaller house, well it seemed to make sense, didn't it? Took all my old bits and bobs, and threw a lot of stuff out. I've got a loft full of pictures and records, old seventy-eights. Some were our May's.

May Yes, I want them buggers back.

Annie I worked on an industrial estate for three years, and then did a bit of cleaning up at school ... I enjoyed that, it was a good gossip.

May I never went to the doctor's.

Harry Their Annie said she should go private.

May I'm going in for some tests. I mean I've been living with this for years. But it's getting bad now. I'm going to see Mr Nish. He's a Pakistani, he's nice. He says I'll feel a different woman when I've had it.

Annie I've told her she won't be a woman, there'll be nowt left.

May She allus looks on the black side.

Harry Twenty-five years!

May Don't mind me.

Harry Twenty-five years.

May And he's never once bought me a red rose.

Harry And it don't seem a day too much ...

May He's there, our Paul.

Paul enters. He is twenty-four. Smart, trendy, obviously a student, but smart not hippy. Tosh is also there. He is same age, with long hair, maybe back across his face. He is wearing a large leather jacket with a Saxon or Def Leppard T-shirt underneath

Tosh Are you dancing?

Paul Not with you.

Tosh How's it going?

Paul Fine.

Tosh Fine?

Paul Don't start telling me that I've changed, Tosh, or I'll die ...

Tosh Thy hasn't lost thee accent then?

Paul (*mocking*) Eee baar gumm, have I heck.

Tosh I thought tha might be lah-di-dah!

Paul Still at t' pit?

Tosh No, I'm a lawyer now.

Paul How's mi dad doing down t' pit?

Tosh It's killing him. He thinks he's still twenty-five. Tha wants to get a job down t' pit. It's smashing.

Paul Touch of irony, eh?

Tosh I read books and all.

Paul I know. Will tha get off my back. I'm still the same.

Tosh Oh ar, I forgot.

Paul Still into Heavy Metal?

Tosh No ... Val Doonican. I've still got all his albums.

Paul Will tha stop bull-shitting?

Tosh What? Bull-shitting, did tha actually say bull-shitting? Tha want a pint?
Paul No, I'll have half.
Tosh S'up wi' thee?
Paul Nothing.
Tosh Have a pint.
Paul No.
Tosh Yes.
Paul No.
Tosh Tha'll have a pint.
Paul I don't want one. I'll just have half.
Tosh I'm not ordering an half in here, they'll think I'm going low.

As they speak Annie walks over bringing a tray of sausage rolls

Annie Here you are, you two, big growing lads. You two buggers. Allus been friends, haven't you? All your lives? Allus been friends, I love you both, I do. Hey, I think that trifle's too alcoholic.

Annie leaves them

Tosh Be a right bloke have a pint. I can drink ten pints and still drive home.
Paul I bet I could drink a hundred.
Annie (*to May*) He's with Tosh.
May They've allus been mates.
Tosh Tha funny.
Paul I know.
Tosh Not funny ha ha, just funny.
Paul Don't look at me like that, Tosh, I know what you're thinking.
Tosh Oh tha's a mind-reader and all, is tha?
Paul I'll have a half.

May, Harry and Annie form a tableaux

May Mr Nish, the consultant, says when I've had it done my nerves won't be half as bad. He says I'll be able to throw the tablets away. Thank God for that; I've been living on 'em for years, there's that many tablets in me, sometimes when I dance you can hear me rattling.

They break the tableaux

   Annie goes

Harry Come and sit down, you silly bugger.
May I'm having a great time. Where's our Paul?
Harry He's with Tosh.
May They're good mates.

   Annie arrives with a bottle of Bailey's Irish Cream

Annie I've just won a bottle of Bailey's Irish Cream in the raffle.

   Kay enters

Paul moves across the stage with Tosh, and meets Kay, Kay is twenty-four, very attractive, whorish, stilettos, over-dressed for the occasion

Kay Oooh, stranger. Your mam's let you come out then?
Paul Got to be in bed soon though.
Kay What is it, a lemonade and a wine gum?
Paul Sommat like that ... How's it going?
Kay Married, now, you know. Two kids.
Paul What's it like? Married life?
Kay It has its moments.
Tosh She married Keith Jackson, he works wi' me.
Kay You look well.
Paul Good livin'.
Kay Is there a woman in your life?
Paul Ish!
Kay Wedding bells?
Paul No! Funny, every time I come home I meet somebody who's just got married, or having kids. Next thing you know Tosh'll be married.
Tosh I'm off.

Tosh moves away

Kay I doubt it.
Paul Ouch, you bitch.
Kay I know, aren't I wicked?
Paul You look good. Slimmer.
Kay You allus said nice things.
Paul I meant them.
Kay Made me feel good.
Paul I'm good with words.
Kay Not very good with bra straps though.
Paul I've got better.
Kay Had some practice then?
Paul A bit. Anyway. Nice to see you. Hope the family is OK, say hello to your mam n' dad.
Kay I will ...
Paul Yeh.
Kay See you ...
Paul Yeh.

She pecks him

Kay You smell nice ...
Paul See you ...

Paul leaves Kay, she watches him go. He turns, walks to Annie, Harry and May

Annie He's not married, got a career, hasn't he May?
May I was married twenty-five years ago today.
Harry If I'd've killed May instead of marrying her I'd've been a free man ten years ago.

May He's courting. What's she called?

Harry Sommat bloody odd.

Annie What she called, Paul, your girl-friend?

Paul She's not my girl-friend, she's a friend who's a girl. Cherry.

Harry Cherry! Where the bloody hell do they get 'em from?

May We've not met her yet.

Annie We're just telling 'em how well you've done.

Paul Oh yeh.

Annie He's done . . . sommat else, what is it?

Paul An MA. I've had a few years off.

Annie I don't know what the bloody hell it is but it's sommat intelligent.

May He's a bit reserved, is our Paul.

Harry He's like May.

May Hey you, he gets his brains from my side of the family.

Harry Does he, bloody hell!

May He's got it all up here, haven't you, kid?

Paul So they say.

May See.

Paul I'm not sure where they've come from must be all that boiled fish.

May I used to give him boiled fish, mi mam swore by it.

Paul I hated it.

May I made him sleep on a board, strengthen his back.

Harry He gets all his talents from me, he gets his moodiness from you.

Annie Yes he does, May, you're moody.

May Oh bloody hell, listen who's talking.

Paul Is everybody OK for a drink?

Annie I'm fine . . . I've had too much I think.

Paul Dad?

Harry No, I'm OK. He fancied himself as a goalie, can you remember?

Paul Oh spare us.

May He thought he was Gordon Banks.

Harry (*calling*) Tosh Tosh . . . come over here.

Tosh What's up, has he bought a pint?

Harry Listen to this.

Tosh comes over and listens

Our Paul fancied himself as a goalkeeper for the local team, and I went to watch him, first time I'd seen him play, and he was jumping about, and he had the gloves and all the bloody rigmorole, and I said to Mr Shaw on the touchline, the bloke who ran the team, I said, what's the score, he says we're losing twenty-four nil, your young 'un's let twenty-four in.

May He let twenty-four in.

Paul I looked brilliant.

Harry I could have buried myself on the touchline.

Paul I was good at diving, I liked to dive.

Harry After the ball had gone in the net.

Paul I don't think it was twenty-four.

Tosh No, more like thirty-four.

Paul (*to the audience*) It was actually seventeen nil. Our family has a tendency to exaggerate.

Harry I don't understand about him having brains. He used to forget whether they were playing at home or away. He once walked all the way to Moorthorpe and when he got there they were playing at Upton.

Paul I only played because you wanted me to, Dad.

Annie I can remember, he used to play in our garage with his Action Man.

Tosh I didn't know thy had an Action Man.

Paul Oh no . . .

Tosh An Action Man? Did it have real hair?

Harry But I'll say this, I only know one other man who's got an MA and that's old Mr Sawyer, Headmaster at the Grammar School. He's the only other one I know.

Tosh Did it have real hair or plastic hair?

Paul It was bald.

May BA. Bloody Awkward, that's what he's been all his life.

Annie And MA. Moody Article.

Paul Oh my family . . .

Annie I've seen Kay Cooper in here tonight, she's married with two kids. Have you seen her? She looks smashing.

Paul No, I've not seen her.

Harry (*shouting across to someone*) Tom? Tom, come and meet our Paul. I've told you about him. Come and meet him. We don't see a lot of him . . . Come and meet him . . .

Music: "Night and Day"

May Listen what they're playing, let's get up, Harry.

Harry I'll get up, what is it?

Annie "Night and Day".

May Come on, Paul, you get up wi' your mam.

Paul I'd rather not.

Annie Go on.

May Come on, you're not that shy.

Harry Get up with her.

Paul I can't dance.

May Follow me, I'll lead, you follow me.

Annie Course you can dance, anybody can.

Paul I'm like a board, honest I am.

Annie Go and dance with your mam.

Paul No.

Harry Go on, bloody hell.

Tosh Go on, Action Man.

Paul I haven't got a clue what to do.

Tosh Go on, you fart.

May Just follow me . . .

Paul and May begin to dance. May dances well but Paul is clumsy and she takes him around the floor while she sings the entire song. During this, a

*collage of events takes place: Annie and Harry look on and call out to Paul;
Tosh laughs and,* UL *in a pose, Kay stands with the wind machine lifting
her skirt, showing her legs in suspenders; Paul cannot help but look at Kay.
Altogether, it's a nightmarish vision*

Annie He's as stiff as a board, drag him around, May.
Harry He's made sommat for hissen.
Tosh Go on, Paul . . . go on.
Annie He's got worse since Blackpool.
Kay Smile, Paul, relax and smile.
Harry Don't watch your feet.
Kay Ring me up, Paul, I'm in the book give me a ring, I'm under Jackson,
  K. Jackson.
Harry He's gerring it.
Annie I think he was better at football.

The cast, with the exception of May and Paul, sing along with the record

  Annie, May, Harry and Tosh exit, clearing all items from the stage

*The music fades. The Lights crossfade to give an outdoor night effect. Paul and
Kay are outside in the car park*

Kay We didn't have much time to talk in there, did we?
Paul No, not really.
Kay How long are you staying up at home for?
Paul Not long if I can help it.
Kay Oh.
Paul Where's the husband?
Kay Tosh's had to take him back. He drinks too much.
Paul So you're all on your own?
Kay 'Fraid so. We should have a chat, you know, Paul. About the old
  times. We had some laughs.
Paul We did.
Kay I'll never forget the things we used t' get up to. The pictures are very
  clear in my mind.
Paul Indelibly inked?
Kay If you say so. You know, I feel like I know you but you seem like a
  complete stranger.
Paul You look lovely, Kay. I could eat you.
Kay I've got all the right bumps that's all.
Paul I better get off home.
Kay I thought you might have lost your accent?
Paul I've lost everything but . . . How are you getting home?
Kay Walk.
Paul Give you a lift if you want?
Kay Got a car?
Paul Second-hand Allegro.
Kay Can I trust you, Paul? Just me and you in a car, we've got a history,
  you know?

Paul and Kay exit

Music: "Night and Day". *The Lights change, the music fades, it is the next morning*

Paul, May and Harry enter, with chairs. May has a newspaper

May We had a great night, didn't we, we had a good night.
Harry We did.
May What time did you get in? I was still awake at half-twelve and there was no sign of you. What were you up to?
Paul Went round to Tosh's.
Harry Told you.
May That's what your dad said.
Harry Have a good night?
Paul Yeh.
May It was a good night. Our Annie enjoyed it, I think she was drunk.
Harry No wonder with that bloody trifle.
May I've got mi Bingo to do. Three numbers, I only want three numbers.
Harry There's probably another three thousand people all wanting three numbers. Anybody want a cuppa?
Paul I don't know why you read that paper.
Harry It's your mother.
May I like to do the Bingo.
Paul It's mindless.
May Forty thousand you can win. I don't think that's mindless. A woman in Rotherham won it last week, it's getting nearer.
Harry Your mother and Bingo!
Paul It wants burning.
May I read the stars and do the Bingo that's all I read in it, I don't look at page three, and then we use it to start the fire.
Harry Cartoons are the best thing in it.
May What are you gunna have for your dinner?
Paul What is there?
May Cheese and egg, like you like it, or fry up. Or cold ham and some sausage rolls.
Paul What else is there?
May I thought you liked cheese and egg?
Paul I did. I might have chinese, skip dinner have something later.
May What do you want a chinese for?
Paul Because I like it.
May It's rubbish to me.
Paul (*indicating the newspaper*) So is that. But you still read it.
Harry Look out.
May What is it that you say about us? Chops with everything, he says we have chops with everything.
Paul Chips, Mother, Chips. It's a play.
May We don't have chips with everything. We don't have chips with cheese and egg, do we Harry?

Harry No, and we don't have chips with chips.
May We have tea with everything.

May hits Paul with the paper and then she exits

The Lights change

Paul (*addressing the audience*) I could just about stand it at home for a day; it was worse than being in San Quentin. My every move was monitored by mi mother, I could actually see the walls of the house getting bigger and bigger, trapping me with them. So I would make some feeble excuse about having to go back to London to go to the library or to see Cherry.

The Lights change

May enters with a dustpan and brush

Paul is about to leave

May Are you going?
Paul I can't work at home any more, Mam.
May I've bought you some of that packaged chinese stuff, I thought you liked it.

The Lights change. May is sweeping the floor

Paul (*to the audience*) And I would leave with a lump in my throat. And as I left I would see my mother sweeping the carpet, sweeping every little speck of dust from the carpet, every piece of toast that dropped on that carpet made a sound to her like a bomb going off . . . I saw the veins in her knarled hands grasping at the Beta-ware . . . It was her life, her creativity, "cleanliness is next to Godliness", she would say, and I left with a real sense of freedom and breath of fresh air, and I left them with whatever problems they had. She never heard my goodbye, she was still sweeping the carpet.

Paul leaves. As he does Mrs Potter and Annie stand in spotlights

Harry despairs at May

Mrs Potter She's having it done then.
Annie What?
Mrs Potter The operation? When's she go in?
Annie About a month.
Mrs Potter Well tell her if she's in need of anything while she's in, to give me a shout.
Annie I'll tell her.
Mrs Potter I know we haven't always got on, but if she wants helping out she knows where I am.
Annie Thanks.
Mrs Potter The sister-in-law had it done. Knocked her up and all very bad. She was never the same again. Knocks the stuffin' out of you so they say.

Mrs Potter exits

Annie (*to the audience*) Everyone had our May's operation on their minds but no-one spoke of it. I busied myself by cleaning out the loft and putting all my seventy-eights into boxes. I thought I'd give them to her when she came out.

Harry She'll be all right once she's been in.

Annie She decided to decorate the house before she went in, so as it would be spick and span when she came out. She wall-papered from top to bottom.

Harry She's going round the bloody bend.

Annie I told her she was barmy.

Harry You can tell her but she doesn't bloody listen.

Music: Doris Day singing "Que Sera Sera"

Harry, May and Annie leave

The Lights change. Paul takes a seat DL

During the following, a hospital bed is brought on UL *and May enters and gets into the bed*

Paul (*to the audience*) Deep down I knew it was a chance to see Kay again so . . . I dragged myself back up home for six days when mi mam had her hysterectomy. Apparently there was something malignant inside her, and this should sort it out. I hate going to hospitals they make me feel ill . . . It was the first time in twenty-seven years that mi dad had been left in the house on his own. He was lost, utterly. He'd come home from work, breathless, and wheezing and sit for three hours on the back-step chopping firewood. He chopped enough firewood to keep the entire Western civilization in firewood for the next fifty years. Then he would dust around the house, listing things as he did them; "The brasses", "The window ledges", "Wash the lino". Whenever he spoke he sounded like mi mother, she had him well trained. And then at night we'd sit by the fire, and like Beckett and James Joyce we'd exchange silences . . . All the while I kept thinking, this man is my dad . . . He would tell me about the "good old days" about the great times he and mi mam had had together, he loved mi mam so much, but for some reason he never ever told her . . .

During the following, while Paul continues to speak to the audience, May is wheeled C. *The Lights are still dark*

(*Slowly walking over to the bed*) When we went to see her she looked like a piece of meat, like a dead pig on a slab all dressed in pink. She was still under the anaesthetic.

The Lights change. May is asleep

(*To May*) Brought some Lucozade. More goodness in one orange so they say. One pound ten for that . . . And some grapes. Mi dad's parking the car. Should be here in an hour. You all right? . . . Asleep.

Paul grabs a chair, sits at the foot of the bed, looks around, eats some of his mother's grapes, and then has a drink of Lucozade

Harry comes in

Asleep.

Harry Oh. Still under.

Harry sits next to Paul at the foot of the bed

Paul Wanna grape?

Harry Do you think she'll be all right?

Paul Yeh.

Harry Good. Smells funny, doesn't it?

Paul Good view though.

Silence

Harry We don't often get time to talk, do we?

Paul Not often.

Harry You know I don't understand what it is that you do.

Paul I write reviews, articles for magazines—films, music—try and flog 'em.
   I get expenses.

Harry Sounds interesting.

Paul And I sign on.

Harry You're not wasting a good education then?

Paul Was that supposed to be a joke?

Harry How's Cherry?

Paul On and off at the moment.

Harry Are we ever gunna see her?

Paul Dunno. Another grape?

Silence

Harry Weather's smashing for November.

Paul Snow forecast.

Harry Is it?

Paul According to the radio.

Harry Oh dear.

Paul She'll need to rest when she comes out. She's never done anything
   interesting, has she?

Harry Everything's ready for her when she gets back.

Paul Another grape?

Harry You can go, you know, if you want. You don't have to stop here. I
   mean if you've got sommat to do.

Paul I'm fine.

Harry There's another hour.

Paul No ... it's nice and warm.

Harry She'll be all right.

Paul Yeh.

Harry Tough as old boots.

Paul She works too hard. Never relaxes.

Harry Thanks for cooking. I'm useless. That Italian thing was lovely. I've
   never had that before, what was it?

Paul Tagliatelle.
Harry Smashing that.
Paul Yeh?
Harry Yeh.
Paul I saw it in the dustbin, Dad, I saw that you'd thrown it in the dustbin.
Harry Not all of it.

Black-out. Music: "Blue Tango", during which the hospital bed is struck

May and Harry exit. Kay appears in a spotlight wearing a fetching red dress

Kay (*to the audience*) Yeh I'm happy, aren't I, I'm satisfied. I've got two little kids and a husband who knocks me about. I've got a mortgage and a microwave, I'm happy. I mean it, very happy. But I'm not excited, not anymore, I feel like I've done all there is to do, my life is over. I don't feel nervous anymore, like something special is going to happen, that's been taken out of me, the boredom, the nappies, the routine, has beaten that out of me. So it was a strange thing, but I knew it was going to happen sooner or later ... I could feel excitement running through my veins again. He was my hero, my very own Milk Tray man, I knew that I was looking at him through a soft focus, I'm not that stupid ... but I had to have him. I wanted to eat him. He was like a big red shiny apple, fresh and unspoilt and I wanted to sink my teeth into his flesh, I wanted to bite him, and I wanted him to want me. He was a big, red rosy apple and I wanted to eat him ... We met in the pub on Wednesday, Keith was on Afters.

The Lights change

Paul She seemed extra-special now, she seemed to be more of a woman ... I couldn't help myself, she cast this web over me. Christ, I talk such bullshit.
Kay Keith would have killed us both if he ever found out but it seemed to be the most wicked thing in the world.
Paul I'd been at the hospital all day.
Kay We had a few drinks ... I had to know.
Paul It was like being caught in an avalanche.
Kay Very cramped and sweaty.
Paul In the back of an Allegro.

Kay and Paul tango upstage behind the set

We hear comic orgasmic noises

Suddenly, Paul appears, holding his back. Kay follows him

Oh mi back. I've got cramp in mi back.
Kay Are you OK?
Paul Yeh. Sorry. Sorry, Kay.
Kay Well, was it what you expected?
Paul Fourteen years I've dreamt of that, Kay, and now? Sorry. I should never have done it. I feel awful.
Kay Not as awful as me, I got mi leg stuck.

Paul Oh, what have I done. You shouldn't have led me on, Kay.

Kay It takes two to tango.

Paul I shouldn't have ever seen you again, I shouldn't have ... I've got no will power.

Kay You could have said no, Paul, you could have gone home.

Paul In a car, in the back of a car? Oh my God.

Kay Stop being so bloody melodramatic. It was just a passing moment. I don't love you, Paul, but I had to have one moment's excitement.

Paul But that's the point, Kay.

Kay What is? What are you on about?

Paul I love you.

Kay Rubbish!

Paul I do, I always have. You've always been in my head.

Kay Paul? Don't!

Paul I mean it. God, I mean it. I can't get rid of you. You're there, haunting me all the time. Oh, it shouldn't have been like this, Kay.

Kay It didn't mean anything.

Paul I can't ever see you again!

Kay Don't flatter yourself. I love my family, Paul. I love 'em, this was just an electric shock to remind me that I'm still alive.

Paul I should never have done it.

Kay Don't worry about it, Paul. You'll get over it. I got over you ...

Paul I was so pathetic.

Kay You were OK given the circumstances.

Paul Don't tell anybody, Kay. Please?

Kay Don't worry I'm not likely to tell your mam, am I?

Paul I'm sorry ... I should never have done it.

Kay Come on, we'll get some fish and chips, make a night of it.

Black-out. Music: "Bali Hai"

Paul and Kay exit. May and Annie enter

The Lights come up. Annie is smoking. May is highly-strung and nervous

Annie Fancy striking. He should go back to work. What are you going to live on? It's every man-Jack for hissen. I bet them union leaders are getting sommat.

May Harry's allus stood by the union. He'll not change now.

Annie They want shooting, all them bloody pickets. They're stopping decent blokes from working.

May For God's sake put a sock in it.

Annie Look at you, it's getting you down again is this strike, you'll end up in hospital again.

May Just shut up, our Annie, before you go too far.

Annie Police are only doing their jobs.

May He says he's not crossing that line, he says, he'll join 'em. He's not working. I don't care if it makes me badly, he's not working. We can't let her beat us, she can't beat the Yorkshire miners, never will she. Mi dad stood by the union and Harry is.

Annie She'll beat 'em, you daft sod, she's got a bloody plan.

May They'll all come out, all of 'em. They'll all come out and support the Yorkshire miners, she'll never beat them buggers, not as long as she's got an hole in her arse ...

Annie It's on telly, you can see 'em all causing trouble.

May They don't show it all.

Annie I could throw stones at the pickets.

May And I'll throw stones through your bloody windows. I didn't vote for 'em.

Annie I did.

May You voted for that bloody lot?

Annie I bloody did, Labour's never done owt for me.

May Get out of this house.

Annie It'll go on forever this strike.

May Get out, Annie.

Annie You'll make yourself bad again.

May I don't care!

Annie Do you think they'll win? You're livin' in a bloody dream world.

May Annie, get out of this bloody house. You're a silly sod, never vote for them, ever, whatever happens, never, mi dad told me that. He lost his bloody lungs down the soddin' pit. Get out, Annie, I mean it.

Annie You'll finish up in Stanley Royd, you will.

May Get out.

Annie You're just like mi dad, three sheets to t' wind.

May I don't want to talk to you.

Annie You drive 'em all away. Our Paul dunt come home like he should because of your bloody tantrums. You're bloody evil, if you'd 've treated him like a proper lad he'd think more of you ... Where is he when you want him?

May Don't you bloody talk to me about kids. You don't know what it's bloody like. You should have had some kids when you had a chance instead of thinking you and Roy were Lord and Lady Muck.

Annie I hope this strike lasts forever, I do. I hope you never have any money, and don't be coming to me for a bloody hand-out because my door will be shut.

May I'll have all the bloody things back from mi mam's that you've been hoarding and all.

Annie Well, you'll have to come and get 'em then. Because I'm not bringing 'em up here. I'll not come up here again until you're dead.

May You're a bloody worm, Annie Parker, get out of my sight.

Annie You're evil you are. Evil.

May and Annie are in tears. Black-out

May and Annie exit

Mrs Potter enters carrying a placard which reads "COAL NOT DOLE", Tosh and Harry stand upstage

The Lights come up

Tosh Come January we'd been out nearly a year.

Mrs Potter Leave 'em alone, you bullies.

Harry We're fighting for us jobs, you silly sods.

Mrs Potter They're not from round here, them police.

Tosh Shit for brains.

Harry Get a PROPER JOB.

Tosh I'll bite your head off, you wimps. Humour was a bit thin on the ground.

Mrs Potter You bloody puppets.

Tosh We built three snowmen outside the pit gates.

Harry We put bits of coal for eyes and nose.

Mrs Potter The police sat there in their Range Rover looking at 'em smiling.

Tosh One of 'em says, is it your own work? I says yeh.

Mrs Potter And then the police ran into our snowmen. You bullies.

Harry Smashed down the end one.

Tosh I called him Derek.

Harry Smashed down the other one.

Tosh That was his wife, Doreen.

Mrs Potter Then they smashed into the middle one. He was the son. We called him Paul.

Harry And the Range Rover stopped, they jolted forward in their seats.

Mrs Potter You're not smiling now.

Tosh We'd built the middle 'un around a concrete post. You bastards.

Mrs Potter They'll never go back.

Harry She'll never shut Kirkby pit.

Tosh There's two hundred years of coal down there.

Mrs Potter How much are you getting in over time?

Harry She'll never shut Kirkby.

Tosh Why don't you get a man's job. Yes, come on, pal, just me and you. I'm six feet ten of insanity.

Mrs Potter Get back down south.

Harry She'll never shut Kirkby.

Music: "Moonlight Serenade". The Lights fade slowly to a spotlight on Paul who walks slowly DR *to address the audience*

Harry, Tosh and Mrs Potter exit. May enters during the following

Paul (*to the audience*) I knew sooner or later that things would come to a head wi mam and dad. I felt like I was betraying myself if they didn't. I didn't come home all year during the miners' strike, I couldn't face the obscenity of it, they'd been ripped apart. And I couldn't run the risk of seeing Kay. So I phoned and listened to mi mam talk nonsense about politics, and mi dad get all worked up in the background. I made the mistake of telling them I was playing in a pub band, I was livin' with Cherry, and I didn't have a "proper job". As far as mi mam and dad were concerned I was now a Martian.

The Lights change

May When are we gunna see her then?
Paul Who?
May Sherry. You hardly come home as it is.
Paul Cherry.
May Three years now, we don't know a thing about her. Is she black, white, red, green? Where's she from, what's she like?
Paul She's all those things and more.
May I wonder about you sometimes, you're mucky, you smell, you never look smart. I didn't bring you up not to have a shave. I thought when you came she could have come, let us have a look at her.

Harry enters from the kitchen. He is older, slower

Harry Bloody Cherry, what sort of name is that?
May I bet he takes bloody drugs.
Paul This is why I don't ask her up.
May Why what's up with us?
Harry (*with a sense of irony*) There's nowt wrong wi rate folks.

Paul is exasperated by his parents

Paul (*starting to move into gear*) You two, it's like Torquemada, it's like the bloody Inquisition. You want to know everything, and when you find out all you do is criticize.
May You've never told us about her.
Paul I've never been able to. I can't talk to you about myself, to you I'm an object. I know you worship me, but I've never felt like a person with you and mi dad, only ever in my head.
May You can talk to us about anything.
Harry We're broadminded, me and your mam.
Paul I can't, that's where you're wrong.
May Oh we're wrong again.
Paul See?
May Wrong again.
Harry I'm bloody fed up of being wrong. I was wrong for supporting Scargill, according to you, I was wrong not eating Italian shite, I was wrong for making you play football, you're the one who's wrong, you're the one who's not got a bloody job, and six years at bloody college, while I've been coughing mi knackers up——
May Hey, steady . . .
Harry —I bet there isn't a more educated bloke at the soddin' dole office.
Paul I've got a job. I'm doing what I want to do.
May He's a disgrace.
Paul Jesus . . . You're so limited.
May Stop swearing in this house, this is my house, I don't want any bloody swearing.
Harry That's all they do that lot, bloody swear.
May He's a disgrace.
Paul I'm twenty-eight years old, I do what I want!
May You look a bugger.

Harry I'm ashamed of him, I am. Ashamed of him.

Paul God help us!

May I'll tell you why we haven't seen her, this bloody Cherry.

Paul Go on then, know all, go on then, tell us why?

May Because he's ashamed of where he comes from.

Paul Don't talk rubbish.

May He is.

Paul Mother, you talk bloody rubbish.

Harry You're a bloody wash-out.

May You mark my words, he's afraid we'll show him up, get in his way, like he said we did at that graduation. Well I'll tell you sommat: I didn't want to go and stand about with that bloody type anyway, set o' bloody farts.

Harry They're pathetic that lot. Set o' bloody snobs.

May We're not good enough for her.

Paul is bursting. He half means this

Paul All right, yes, I don't bring her home because I'm ashamed: because every time I come into this bloody house, there's arguing, and I can't sit on that, or have I got clean on? or I've dropped a crumb, are my socks clean, have I had a shave today? And you two are at each other's throats all the time. Do you honestly think everybody in the world shouts at each other all the time, do you, honestly? Do you think reasonable conversation is dead? That because somebody has a different opinion to you, Mother, it makes them less of a person. Do you——

May Look at him shouting.

Paul I'm shouting to make sure you hear me, because we are now on different planets, I'm on Mars and you two are on bloody Pluto.

Harry Stop swearing at your mother.

Paul And why should I bring somebody somewhere where they aren't wanted. Now . . . That's it. I've finished. I've had my say. Sorry. But . . . I had to say it. Sorry.

Silence

May Well, if that's how you feel about us you had better leave, and not come back.

Paul Jesus, this is a nut-house, I can't talk rationally to you. I was just getting it off my chest.

May And I'm getting this off mine, let him go.

Paul I will.

May Go.

Paul I will.

May Go. Get.

Paul If I walk out of here, you'll never see me. I'll never come back, I swear to God.

May Go.

Harry There's no need for all this upset.

Paul I mean it, Mother.

May And I bloody mean it, you're dealing with your mother here, not some shit-arse from university. If that's the way you feel, go. Get out.

Harry I said this would happen.

May It's you and all, not just me, he's talking about, you and all. Let him go!

Silence

Paul Right.

Paul leaves

Silence

Harry (*in an outburst, through tears*) I could kill you, I could, I could kill you. Oh God ... that's my lad ... My lad ... I could swing for you ...

May Let him go ...

Harry This family. This bloody rotten family.

They freeze. Silence. The Lights change

Annie enters

Annie (*to the audience*) Our May had got mi dad's streak in her; she didn't mind hurting people even if it meant hurting herself. She never wanted our Paul to leave like that.

May He can go, I'm not bothered what he does.

Annie She turned the hurt in on herself, like someone pulling their own teeth, she enjoyed the agony. She let it fester inside her. Arguing with our Paul must have torn her up inside, he was all she lived for.

May He never rings me these days.

Annie I never saw her, I stayed at home and knitted and on a weekend I'd still go and keep Roy's grave nice and tidy. I'd often see Kay Cooper, she'd had another little boy ... and was looking well.

Annie exits

The Lights change. Music: "April in Paris" Harry and May address the audience

Harry In nineteen eighty-six we went to Paris. We went on a bus trip.

May Paris was breathtaking.

Harry We saw everything, the Arch de Triumph, Louvre.

May We walked by the Seine.

Harry I was nearly in seine.

May That's supposed to be a joke.

Harry Bonjour, May.

May Bonjour, Harry.

Harry We picked up a bit of French.

May Bloody hell!

Harry We bought French bread.

May We saw the *Mona Lisa*.

Harry I saw the moaner May.

May Pathetic, he is, he's pathetic with jokes.

Harry And wished I'd taken redundancy ten years ago. We had fifteen thousand. By the time we'd paid for the house there wasn't much left; but I felt free, I felt like I'd got the sun on my back. I felt twenty years younger. We walked all over Paris, made ourselves bad with it.

May My arthritis was bad. But it was a time for getting to know each other again.

A burst of "April in Paris"

> *May and Harry exit. Then they return: Harry with an ironing board and iron, May with a sheet, and they begin to attempt to fold the sheet*

Harry We were like little kids. I missed the pit like a hole in the head.

May He's a liar . . . for the first year he never stopped talking about the pit; at night he'd be sat up in bed wide-awake waiting for the shift to start.

Harry We worked as a team on the domestic front. I used t' say that May lets me make all the big decisions, like will we have nuclear fuel, or should we be in the Common Market, and I let her make all the small decisions, like where are we going for our holidays or how much are we gunna spend at the supermarket. (*He begins to iron*)

May I never saw our Annie, there was just the two of us. And we hardly went out.

Harry I started to potter about the house doing DIY. I became an expert. I could build a wardrobe in a telephone box, and May would have made a great under manager; she had me working harder than Mr Poole ever did. Have you had a tablet?

May I'll tek one.

Harry You should have one after every meal it says on the packet.

May Do you allus do everything you're supposed to?

Harry No.

May Well then.

Harry Oh, that's OK then.

May Iron the corners.

Harry I am.

May You're not.

Harry I am.

May I can see from here that you're not.

Harry Do you want to iron 'em?

May No, mi hands are bad . . .

Harry Well shut up then, moan a lot.

May That's told me.

Harry Put a record on.

May You put one on.

Harry Only if you smile, you foul pig, who do you want?

May Glen Miller. I'm smiling.

Music: "Elmer's Tune"

> *Harry exits with the ironing board and iron. May clears the chairs. Harry returns with a lawn-mower. Tosh enters and sees him*

Tosh Get that grass cut.
Harry Na then.
Tosh How's retirement, tha like it?
Harry Fantastic. If I had my time agen I'd be a gardener.
Tosh I thought tha got hayfever?
Harry That's the only draw-back. How's things going down at work?
Tosh Tha hasn't heard then?
Harry Heard what?
Tosh She's shuttin' Kirkby pit.
Harry Give over.
Tosh They've given us an offer, take the money or a job at another pit. Well, that makes sense, dun't it, in a shrinking industry? All the best jobs have gone.
Harry When's she shuttin' it?
Tosh A fortnight.
Harry Well, they might shut the Welfare an' all, tha knows, social money came from t' pit into the Welfare . . . be no dancin' then.
Tosh Ar. Bastards. Ninety-five per cent of what Scargill said was right.
Harry What's tha gunna do?
Tosh Dunno.
Harry Bloody hell, she's shutting Kirkby. (*He sneezes*)
Tosh Bless you.
Harry Thanks.
Tosh I might start a window-cleaning job, tha knows, set mi own firm up.
Harry Well there's one thing, you won't need a ladder.
Tosh I'll need a bucket though.
Harry Fifty years ago they were crying out for miners. Essential works order, now we're on the scrap-heap. Your young lads'll not get much.
Tosh No, I might go and see Bruce Springsteen with my redundancy money.
Harry Hey Tosh . . . I feel right sorry for you.
Tosh Ar . . . I do. How's laddo?
Harry We never hear from him from one week to the next.
Tosh Ar well . . . Cut your grass for a fiver.
Harry Bugger off.
Tosh I mean it.
Harry Is tha joking?
Tosh No . . .
Harry Go on then.

Tosh takes the mower and exits

The scene changes to Harry and May's home. It is 1988, and it is May's sixtieth birthday

Harry fetches some chairs. May enters. She looks much older and she is wearing slippers and a cardigan over her dress

May Sixty?
Harry Sixty . . .

May Bloody sixty not out. Where's my red roses?

Harry Still in the shop.

May Ay I thought they would be. You're about as romantic as a wood-louse. Never bought me any flowers.

Harry They give me hayfever, you know that.

May Never bought me any.

Harry Bloody sixty.

May And achieved bloody nowt. It all seems to have gone by so quickly. I could roar when I think about it. And I thought we were going to be the folks who lived on the hill.

Harry That was going to be Annie and Roy.

May Arr ... poor old Roy. I wonder what he'd 've been doing now? Sixty? Nowt to look forward to.

Harry We're going away next year, bus trip to Paris.

May I love Paris, sommat about it. I love it.

Harry You're only as old as you feel.

May Nowt to look forward to, it's all behind us now.

Harry We could go into home improvements. You could go around checking up to see if people are cleaning their houses good enough.

May I don't clean my own like I did.

Harry You do too much.

May Bloody sixty, and I've only got two cards.

Harry One better than last year. (*He takes a moment and then addresses the audience*) She's not been too well, to be honest. I think the doctors thought that the operation would catch it, but I don't think it has. She's in terrible pain sometimes. We haven't told anybody. And me? Sometimes I look in the mirror and wonder who I am.

Tosh enters still dressed as for a rock concert. He is carrying a bottle of Remy Martin with the price still on it

Tosh Can I come in? Na then?

May Hey up Tosh, come in, lad.

Tosh Harry!

Harry All right?

Tosh Happy birthday, Mrs H. (*He hands her the bottle of Remy Martin*)

May Oh Tosh ... oh, you shouldn't have.

Tosh It's rate.

May A bottle of brandy, Remy Martin. Int that nice, you've left the price on ...

Harry Thought that counts.

Tosh It's to share really.

May Look at the price, you shouldn't have.

Tosh Care of Mr Sainsbury that. I didn't buy it, he'll not miss one bottle.

May Oh, you little bugger.

Tosh Sixty then? What's it feel like?

May Old.

Harry Fantastic.

Tosh Mi mam's seventy-one in August.

Harry Ar?

May Seventy-one.

Tosh I thought I'd pop round, nowt else to do.

May You can do my windows if you like, while you're here.

Tosh It'll cost you. I'm self-employed now, you know, I don't do owt for nowt.

Paul and Cherry (dressed in a Laura Ashley print) appear at the door

Silence. Everyone is very tense throughout the following scene

Paul Can I come in or what?

Harry Bloody hell!

Cherry (*shyly*) Hello.

Paul Happy birthday, Mam. Have I got the right day?

May What do you want? There's nowt here for you.

Paul I thought this was "home"?

May I thought you were never coming back?

Paul I wasn't.

May Well, what you come for? You're ashamed of us, aren't you?

Harry Give it a miss, May.

May We could be dead for all he's bothered.

Paul Can we come in or what?

Harry Ar bloody hell, get yourselves in.

May Well look at you, you look like a bloody circus. Have you got clean on?

Paul Mother spare us. Tosh?

Tosh Not bad.

Paul Zig?

Tosh Zog.

They shake hands

May Who is this then?

Paul Mam, this is Cherry.

Tosh Cherry?

Cherry Paul's told me all about you, Mrs Hickman.

May I bet he has an' all.

Tosh What sort of a bloody name is that?

May I bet he's told you what a bad pig I've been to him.

Cherry Well, no ... not really.

May Everything we did, we did for him; everything we sacrificed, we sacrificed for him; and then he turned his bloody back on us.

Paul Here, happy birthday. Don't say I never give you owt.

May I don't want anything off you.

Paul Bloody tek it. (*He offers her a rose and a wrapped present: Chanel No. 5*)

Harry Cuppa tea, anybody? May? Cherry? Cuppa tea. I'm allus making tea, Cherry, I mek more tea than Typhoo.

Cherry Yes, please, Mr Hickman ... It's a nice house, Mrs Hickman.

Harry exits

May It should be, all I do is clean it. It should be more than nice.
Cherry I like the wallpaper.
May Blown vinyl, I got it in Wakefield. Oh, Chanel Number Five, Harry.
  He must think we stink, and a red rose. Bloody hell. I've had to wait sixty
  years for that.
Paul I heard about Kirkby. Out of work?
Tosh No, I'm a brain-surgeon now.
Paul Well, you've got the hands for it.
May I'm surprised you remembered where we live.
Cherry We called a month ago.
Paul Nobody in.

Harry enters from the kitchen

Harry We've been away, Yugoslavia. Only cheap. I've got a jar in there,
  Paul, and I can save seventy quid in it in twenty pence pieces. Everytime I
  get one I put it in mi jar. It's mi "going away jar".
Paul Sounds good.
Harry Ay ... Shall I get a bit of cake out, May?
Tosh Ay, get some cherry cake. Soz, couldn't resist that one.
May Has she met Tosh?
Tosh Is that your real name?
Cherry Is Tosh yours?
Tosh No it's Edward, but I feel a bit of a fart being called Edward around
  here.
May He's all rate, aren't you, Tosh?
Paul Don't bother with any food, Dad. I thought we'd go out, I've made
  arrangements for us all to go out.
May I'm not going out.
Cherry We've booked a table.
May I'm stopping in.
Paul Mother ... ?
Harry Come on, May ... he's treating us.
May No, I don't want to go out.
Harry She hardly ever goes out. She's like a fixture, you can't get her out of
  the house. She just sits and listens to the wireless.
May Shut up, you.
Cherry You'll enjoy it, Mrs Hickman.
May How do you know if I'll enjoy it?
Cherry Well ... I thought ...
Harry Come on, May ...
May No ... I've told you.
Paul (*making the effort*) Come on, you foul old swine. I've booked for a
  carvery, now come on. Get ready, let's go out and have a good birthday.
May No ... I'm not going out. I'm not going. I'm staying in this house, this
  is my house, I'm staying in it. Don't think you can come and start
  ordering me about. I'm not going anywhere, I'm not.
Harry May?

May, in tears, begins to make her way out. Tosh stands up

May No, I didn't ask him to come back—he can go back to London for me. Go back where he bloody belongs.

Harry is about to follow her off. The atmosphere is difficult

May exits

Harry She gets all upset, she's not well. She's pleased to see you.

Harry exits

Tosh Anyway . . . I'll get off. Just popped around to see 'em. I keep mi eye on 'em. Funny how things work out, int it? Kay's left her husband, tha knows? Lives with her mam.
Paul No, I didn't know.
Tosh Anyway. Nice to meet you, Cherry. Cheers. I'll get off home, make mi mam a cuppa.

Tosh leaves

Cherry and Paul are left alone

Cherry Is your mum OK?
Paul I told you we shouldn't have come.
Cherry Don't get at me.
Paul It was your bright idea.
Cherry You're joking. I didn't want to trail all the way up here.
Paul I told you, didn't I, like a nut-house. She'll only be crying for the next seven hours.
Cherry I think she's just over emotional.
Paul You can say that agen. God . . . Philip Larkin was right, you know. But I can't desert 'em. They need support from us.
Cherry Hey come on, cheer up . . . Have you got clean underpants on?
Paul No . . .
Cherry Well . . . I'm going to tell your mother.
Paul You would and all.

Harry enters from the kitchen

Harry Sorry about that, kid; your mother's up and down all the time at the minute. You know what she's like. She says she's not going out and I think she means it . . . Sorry.

Silence

Paul Let me have a word wi her?
Harry Come on, Cherry, let's me and you go and get some fresh air in the garden. I'll show you what a pit used to look like.

Harry and Cherry leave

Paul (*calling*) Mam . . . ? Mother . . . ?

Paul exits

Music: "I'll Be With You In Apple Blossom Time". *The lights fade*

Annie slowly enters, and sits R. *She sits alone for a moment, then May enters. It is later the same day. May is wearing a coat—she has simply thrown it on*

Silence

Annie What do you want?
May To see you.
Annie Come for your records back?
May No. Not really.
Annie You can have 'em. There in a box int other room, cracked most of 'em.
May Oh . . . I got your card.
Annie Can't afford a present. Card cost me ninety pence.
May I thought I'd better come and see if you were still alive.
Annie Been bad wi' mi kidneys.
May This house is a tip . . . don't you clean it?
Annie No, I don't bother. I sit here in the dark waiting to die.
May I'll come and clean it for you.
Annie You've no need.
May Our Paul's come home, brought this Cherry.
Annie Oh ay?
May She looks nice. Likes mi house.
Annie That's nice for you.
May He's taking me out to a carvery for mi birthday.
Annie Well, what you come here for?
May Do you want to come?
Annie I've got nowt to wear.
May He says come as you are—I've just thrown mi coat on. Are you coming or not?

Silence for as long as it will hold

Annie Well, I right fancy a dance.
May Well bloody come on then.

Annie exits at speed

Music: "Black Seam" *by Sting*

Harry, Tosh, Paul and Cherry enter slowly. Annie returns, wearing a coat

Annie looks to Paul. The Lights shine on Paul from below, which gives the impression of a shaft of light on a coal seam and, effectively, cuts the stage in two. Slowly, Annie looks at the audience, and, as she does, all the cast begin to dance a modern dance slowly which gives a sinister effect. Paul envelops both his mother and his aunty, the three of them forming a picture, and Paul leads them in a bow

CURTAIN

FURNITURE AND PROPERTY LIST

ACT I

On stage: Nil

Off stage: Shovels **(Harry, Roy)**
Mirror-ball **(Stage Management)**
Picnic-case, rug, etc. **(Harry, Roy)**
Three chairs **(Roy, Annie)**
Pram **(May)**
Dustpan and brush **(May)**
Newspaper **(Harry)**
Sweeping brush **(Tosh)**
Tennis racquet, record album cover, sketch **(Paul)**
Two washing lines, bags of pegs, clothing, net curtains, sheets, pillow cases
   etc. **(Annie, May, Harry)**
Plastic washing basket **(May)**
Letter **(Harry)**

Personal: **Annie:** handbag
May: handbag
Mrs Gillespie: handbag containing a coin
Mrs Potter: lighted cigarette

ACT II

On stage: Three chairs. *On one:* tray of sausage rolls

Off stage: Bottle of Bailey's Irish Cream **(Annie)**
Newspaper **(May)**
Hospital bed. *On it:* sheets, pillows, blanket etc., bottle of Lucozade,
   grapes **(Stage Management)**
Placard reading "COAL NOT DOLE" **(Mrs Potter)**
Ironing board, iron **(Harry)**
Sheet **(May)**
Lawn-mower **(Harry)**
Bottle of Remy Martin **(Tosh)**
Rose, gift-wrapped bottle of Chanel No. 5 **(Paul)**

Personal: **Annie:** lighted cigarette

LIGHTING PLOT

Property fittings required: nil.

Various interior and exterior settings

ACT I

To open: House lights on, dim general lighting on stage

Cue 1	When ready *Fade house lights; crossfade to deep blue night effect*	(Page 1)
Cue 2	**Annie** and **May** exit at speed *Crossfade to wide, diagonal shaft of light*	(Page 2)
Cue 3	Music: "String of Pearls" *Overall bright lighting with spot on mirror-ball*	(Page 3)
Cue 4	**May:** "We were one big family." *Cut spot on mirror-ball*	(Page 4)
Cue 5	**May:** "He's a worm, Roy, but I love him ..." *Crossfade to spot downstage* C	(Page 8)
Cue 6	**Harry:** "... the meaning of the word love." *Black-out, then bring up overall lighting when ready*	(Page 8)
Cue 7	**Annie:** "... I could live without you." *Crossfade to deep blue, bring up spot on* **May**	(Page 9)
Cue 8	**May:** "... on to the common." *Crossfade to bright overall lighting*	(Page 9)
Cue 9	**Annie:** "... back to your mam, shall we?" *Crossfade to spots* UL, C, *and* DR	(Page 11)
Cue 10	**Harry** and **May** leave *Fade spots* UL *and* DR	(Page 11)
Cue 11	Music: Bob Hope's "Thanks for the Memory" *Crossfade to spot upstage on* **Mrs Potter**	(Page 12)
Cue 12	When music has faded *Crossfade to lighting downstage*	(Page 12)
Cue 13	**Mrs Potter** exits *Crossfade to overall lighting*	(Page 12)
Cue 14	**May:** "... what you're saying." *Crossfade to lighting downstage*	(Page 13)
Cue 15	**Annie:** "... without his mother knew about it." *Crossfade to overall lighting*	(Page 14)

Cue 16   **Kay** runs off   (Page 18)
            Crossfade to lighting downstage

Cue 17   **Paul:** ". . . would have to die as well."   (Page 19)
            Crossfade to overall lighting

Cue 18   **Paul:** ". . . into a nervous wreck."   (Page 21)
            Black-out. Bring up overall lighting when ready

Cue 19   **May:** ". . . it's worrying me to death."   (Page 23)
            *Crossfade to follow spot on **Paul**, with dim lighting upstage to
            give overcast effect*

Cue 20   **Paul** exits   (Page 24)
            Cut spot

Cue 21   **Kay** is left alone   (Page 27)
            Fade to Black-out

ACT II

To open: Overall lighting

Cue 22   **Annie, May** and **Tosh** exit   (Page 34)
            Crossfade to night effect

Cue 23   Music: "Night and Day"   (Page 35)
            Crossfade to overall lighting

Cue 24   **May** exits   (Page 36)
            *Crossfade to spot on **Paul***

Cue 25   **Paul:** ". . . or to see Cherry."   (Page 36)
            Crossfade to overall lighting

Cue 26   **May:** ". . . I thought you liked it."   (Page 36)
            *Concentrate lighting on **Paul***

Cue 27   **Paul** leaves   (Page 36)
            *Bring up spots on **Mrs Potter** and **Annie** and increase lighting on
            May*

Cue 28   **Harry, Annie** and **May** exit   (Page 37)
            *Crossfade to spot on **Paul** DL*

Cue 29   **Paul:** "She was still under the anaesthetic."   (Page 37)
            Crossfade to overall lighting

Cue 30   **Harry:** "Not all of it."   (Page 39)
            *Black-out. When ready, bring up spot on **Kay***

Cue 31   **Kay:** "Keith was on Afters."   (Page 39)
            Crossfade to overall lighting

Cue 32   **Kay:** ". . . make a night of it."   (Page 40)
            Black-out. When ready, bring up overall lighting

Cue 33   **May** and **Annie** are in tears   (Page 41)
            Black-out. When ready bring up lighting upstage

Cue 34	**Harry:** "She'll never shut Kirkby."	(Page 42)
	Slow crossfade to follow spot on **Paul**	
Cue 35	**Paul:** "... I was now a Martian."	(Page 42)
	Crossfade to overall lighting	
Cue 36	They freeze. Silence	(Page 45)
	Dim lighting, bring up spots on **Annie** *and* **May**	
Cue 37	**Annie** exits	(Page 45)
	Crossfade to overall lighting	
Cue 38	Music "I'll Be With You in Apple Blossom Time"	(Page 51)
	Dim lighting	
Cue 39	**Annie** looks to **Paul**	(Page 52)
	Reduce overall lighting. Bring up intense shaft of light from below	
	on **Paul**	

EFFECTS PLOT

A licence issued by Samuel French Ltd to perform this play does not include permission to use the Overture and Incidental music specified in this copy. Where the place of performance is already licensed by the Performing Right Society a return of the music used must be made to them. If the place of performance is not so licensed then application should be made to the Performing Right Society, 29 Berners Street, London W1.

A separate and additional Licence from Phonographic Performances Ltd, Ganton House, Ganton Street, London W1 is needed whenever commercial recordings are used.

ACT I

Cue 1	To open *Judy Garland recording of "The Trolley Song"*	(Page 1)
Cue 2	**Annie** and **May** exit at speed *Bing Crosby recording of "Piociana"*	(Page 2)
Cue 3	**Roy:** "... who you were." Pause *Music: "String of Pearls"*	(Page 3)
Cue 4	**Harry:** "It was all we needed." *Music: "Begin the Beguine"*	(Page 6)
Cue 5	**May:** "He's a worm, Roy, but I love him ..." *Music: "Elmer's Tune"*	(Page 8)
Cue 6	**Annie:** "... I could live without you." *Music: Dick Haymes' "You'll Never Know"*	(Page 9)
Cue 7	**Annie:** "... to your mam, shall we?" *Bing Crosby recording of "Piociana", after a while, start wind machine and continue, increasing in intensity*	(Page 11)
Cue 8	**Annie:** "Roy!" *Cut music and wind machine*	(Page 11)
Cue 9	**Harry:** "... those he's left behind." *Wind howling, then decrease slightly and continue*	(Page 11)
Cue 10	**Annie:** "... Roy, Roy, ROY, ROY!" *Crossfade wind effect to Bob Hope recording of "Thanks for the Memory", then fade slowly*	(Page 12)
Cue 11	**May:** "... what you're saying." *Nat King Cole recording of "When I Fall in Love"*	(Page 13)

Cue 12	**Tosh** leaves with **Kay** *Music: "Begin the Beguine"*	(Page 15)
Cue 13	**Paul:** ". . . dancing to old time records. . ." *Music: a slow foxtrot*	(Page 15)
Cue 14	**Tosh** exits *Music: "Volare", then fade slowly*	(Page 19)
Cue 15	**Kay:** "Don't you want it?" *Music: Elvis Presley recording of "Fever"*	(Page 20)
Cue 16	Black-out *Smoke effect. Music: 'Ziggy Stardust'*	(Page 21)
Cue 17	**May:** ". . . it's worrying me to death." *Music: "Moonlight Cocktail"*	(Page 23)
Cue 18	**Paul** exits *Wind blows strongly, heavy rain effect. Continue*	(Page 24)
Cue 19	**Harry:** "Bloody university. Bloody hell." *Fade wind and rain effects. Music: "Face the Music"*	(Page 26)

ACT II

Cue 20	To open *Music: "The Anniversary Waltz"*	(Page 28)
Cue 21	**Harry:** "Come and meet him . . ." *Music: "Night and Day". Continue*	(Page 33)
Cue 22	While **Paul** and **May** dance *Wind machine*	(Page 33)
Cue 23	**Annie, May, Harry** and **Tosh** exit *Fade music and wind machine*	(Page 34)
Cue 24	**Paul** and **Kay** exit *Music: "Night and Day", then fade*	(Page 35)
Cue 25	**Harry:** ". . . but she doesn't bloody listen." *Doris Day recording "Que Sera Sera"*	(Page 37)
Cue 26	**Harry:** "Not all of it." *Music: "Blue Tango"*	(Page 39)
Cue 27	**Kay:** ". . . make a night of it." *Music : "Bali Hai"*	(Page 40)
Cue 28	**Harry:** "She'll never shut Kirkby." *Music: Moonlight Serenade"*	(Page 42)
Cue 29	**Annie** exits *Music: "April in Paris"*	(Page 45)
Cue 30	**May:** ". . . to know each other again." *Burst of "April in Paris"*	(Page 46)

Cue 31 **May:** "Glen Miller. I'm smiling."   (Page 46)
          Music: "Elmer's Tune"

Cue 32 **Paul** exits   (Page 51)
          Music: "I'll Be With You in Apple Blossom Time"

Cue 33 **Annie** exits at speed   (Page 52)
          Music: "Black Seam" by Sting

MADE AND PRINTED IN GREAT BRITAIN BY
LATIMER TREND & COMPANY LTD PLYMOUTH

MADE IN ENGLAND